Living Sober Sucks!

(*but living drunk sucks more*)

2014

Living Sober Sucks

Published by: CW Media, Inc.

Printed in the United States of America by an American owned company.

All inquiries about this book, including interviews, purchases or speaking engagements can be made through email: **booksales@LivingSoberSucks.com**

Please don't bother the Library of Congress Cataloging-in-Publication Data, they're very busy handing out entitlements.

ISBN 10: 0-9842730-0-X
ISBN 13: 978-0-9842730-0-3

Second print run edition.

<u>Dedication:</u>

To Leon and Cele Tuschel.
Without you I wouldn't be here.
I hope to make you both proud.

Dedication Part 2:

I must further acknowledge that this book is dedicated to all the people that listened to my blubbering whiney ass while I was going through my sobering up process. Namely my best buddies Mike, Jeff K, Jeff B, Willie, Barry and all my other drinking buddies that never left me after I sobered up. For my dad who went from being my dad - to being my friend. To my sister Linda who also became a dear friend to me. To LH, "thank you." You didn't try to do it but you ultimately sobered me up. For my friends who spent their personal time reading, editing and discussing this project with me; Dana, Jeff K., Beth, Dr. Modell. I especially must thank my dear friend Jhennifer. That crazy red-haired broad pushed me so hard to write this. I don't think I ever would have finished had it not been for her. To everyone who has visited or contacted me through my website **www.LivingSoberSucks.com** - I am so honored to be part of your lives and to have you as part of mine.

I thank all of you for your patience and love. Had you not cared about me, I never would have sobered up and wrote this. I must also thank all the rotten cocksuckers and motherfuckers that talked bad about me, wouldn't help me become sober, claimed that I would never stay sober, claimed that I would never amount to anything, claimed that I was a pathetic lazy bum. They are the people that kept me motivated to become and stay sober. Unwittingly they pushed me to make good things happen in my life.

Don't underestimate the power of love and the power of anger. Nothing wrong with letting either of those emotions blossom and drive you throughout your life. Don't underestimate your own willpower. You can do it - I did.

Mark A. Tuschel

Contents

5

Introduction:

I owned a timeshare condo in hell. You may ask, "Why would anyone want to own a timeshare condo in hell?" Well, just like most timeshares, you talk yourself into it. At first it seems like a good idea - a fun place to hang out at a great price. But then, just like most timeshares, you get stuck with it and you have to go there whether you want to or not. Then you try to get out of the deal, but you're committed - you're invested too deep, you can't even give the fuckin' thing away. Next thing you know it's costing you more than you ever imagined. This timeshare condo in hell isn't just costing you money (lots of money), it is also costing you your health, your friendships, your relationships with lovers, spouses and family. It will cost you success at work and in your private life. It imposes fees on your emotional stamina, charges you with mental anguish and guilt, makes you compromise your personal integrity, values, your morals, maybe even engulfs you with legal problems and debt. I could go on. Just take my word for it, this timeshare will cost you everything you ever had, you ever accomplished, you ever valued, loved or respected in your life.

America can be a tough country to stay sober in. Abraham Lincoln should have said, "Four score and seven years ago our fathers brought forth on this continent, BEER!" It is a fact that much of our society revolves around drinking. Alcohol is part of our economy, our history, our culture, and our families - that's just the way it is. I would never say that alcohol should be banned or that it's bad. Prohibition didn't work from 1917 to 1929 and it sure ain't gonna work now.

It's okay to drink, it's even okay to get drunk. Many people are capable of being responsible social drinkers - but I am not one of them. I wish I could get drunk, I liked getting drunk, some of the best times I ever had were while I was drunk. I did a lot of things I never would have done sober. Can you believe that an alcoholic would say that? I'm not trying to talk you out of quitting or into having a relapse. My purpose is to speak openly and honestly.

Despite *feeling* that I have been dealt an abundance of bad luck, I realize that I've lived a pretty charmed existence. When I step back to look at my life, I have to admit that I have been blessed with my fair share of good luck. My life is probably far less interesting and exciting than that of oh, say, a celebrity, rock star, porn star, sports hero, really rich person or a Catholic priest. But it is also far more thrilling and rewarding than a lot of others. I have led an unconventional and wild life, filled with numerous high risk activities. However I believe that I am more like the average person than I may want to admit. I feel that my story, what I've been through, why I drank, how I quit drinking and the struggles I face can be helpful to the average drunk. I don't feel special, I probably feel like everybody else that wants to stop drinking. We all have our own story, but we have one thing in common - we're addicts. Whether we're drunks, drug addicts, whatever it is, we're addicted.

I feel that one of my strongest attributes is my ability to accept that where I am today is a result of what I did yesterday. It's a simple way of saying that I am responsible for all of the good and bad choices I have made. It is a fact that other people, unforeseen circumstances and happenings affect our lives, but to steal a phrase, I believe that I reap what I've sown.

The way I went about sobering myself up is not the answer for everyone. My methods, approach and techniques have worked for me and hopefully they will be of benefit to others. I did many things in my recovery that are frowned upon. I will be sharing my philosophies with you, my stages of progress and my techniques to achieving and maintaining sobriety. I have my own views and ideas about recovery and personal growth that don't run in unison with AA and other recovery programs. Don't get me wrong, AA is a life saver for many. Intervention or rehab may be a required starting point for some people. Ultimately it is up to *you* to sober yourself up. Family and friends will make or break you. Choose wisely and carefully who you associate with and who you seek help from. People you trust at first may turn out to be your biggest enemies.

I wonder why I feel so lucky to have been an alcoholic. I wonder how I was able to recover on my own, heal myself and *supposedly* become a better, more rounded person. I wonder how I was able to stay sober while I endured painful experiences, situations that I thought were unfair, the ugliness of reality and cruelties of life that become so vividly clear without the anesthesia of alcohol. I have no superhuman powers; I am nothing special, I am no better than anyone else. The answer to these questions is: *I simply believe in my own willpower.*

I am told that I am a freak of nature because after 32 years of regular, daily, heavy drinking - I sobered up. I did this without going into rehab or treatment, without going to daily or weekly AA meetings, without medications, without substitute drugs or switching addictions, even without the help of the woman I loved, trusted and counted on, my wife of 23 years. I sobered up by using my own sheer willpower, self discipline and an acceptance that *living as an alcoholic is a choice.*

Are there more problems and obstacles in my life now that I'm not drinking? Without hesitation I can answer, "YES!" All of my problems and obstacles seem to have come rushing at me all at once when I finally started living sober. But it is through sober eyes that I am able see how many personal flaws I have. Sobriety has enabled me to attack my flaws and life's difficulties - to work on making the necessary changes and overcome them. Sobriety is helping me win many of the battles in life's game.

When I decided to quit drinking I didn't know that it (sobriety) would end up altering my life so dramatically. I never imagined that I would undertake such a huge transformation in my behaviors. I had no idea how much personal reflection and self-improvement I would end up doing. I also didn't know how painful, difficult and rewarding this would all be. If I would have known this, and had I known how agonizing this would be, I may never have tried.

I won't bullshit you - this won't be easy - in fact it'll be real fucking hard - almost too hard at times. I had thought that quitting drinking would be a piece of cake once I decided to do it. I figured that my life would become wonderful, filled with love and laughter. I imagined how all my friends, family and wife would love me even more. I thought my world would become sunny, bright and filled with joy. Guess what? - I was wrong! It turns out that a lot of things didn't get any better. In fact, people I trusted turned on me and some people don't like me anymore. People that I thought were my friends talked shit about me, tried to undermine what I was trying to do and some even became fearful of me.

Every morning when I wake up and get out of bed, life still shows up, but now I have to face it sober. I expected bigger and better things out of sobriety. Sobriety is nothing like I thought it would be. It is strange. It is not neat and orderly. Life comes at you in unexpected directions at unexpected speeds. Sobriety does not automatically come bearing happiness, friends and love. It is dull and quite often it sucks. For me, that's the reality of sobriety.

Many of your friends and relatives will tell you to just avoid temptation to stay sober. Their words are well-meant and well-intended. But people who have never been an addict can't relate to what we go through. They can't understand what is so hard, what is so painful, why all the agony and temptation? They have lived their life sober. Even social drinkers can't understand - they are able to control their drinking. I enjoy feeling my pain in some strange way. The ups and downs are what make life worth living.

This is my story of how I started drinking, why I drank, what I did to take control of my life and ultimately stop drinking. These

10

are the things that worked for me, as well as the things that didn't work for me. My technique may work better for you than it did for me - I hope it does. My style may not work for you at all. Just the fact that you're reading this and you're willing to try something is a promising sign. I am not a trained therapist; I do not have any formal education with regard to substance and alcohol abuse. While I have taken it upon myself to study about substance abuse and rehab over the past six years, I have mostly learned from my own experience and the experiences of others. I only know what I was able to do for myself. And you will have to do this for yourself. I cannot make you sober. I cannot make your life better. I can only pass along ideas to you and you will have to discover for *yourself* what does or does not work for you.

Living Sober Sucks was written over a three year period of time. I started writing this approximately one year after I sobered up. I wrote many parts during the earliest and most fucked up stages of my recovery (cited as *Journal Entries* in chapter 18). I have put actual dates on the *Journal Entries* because I want to share with you all of the changes and different stages of my thinking during my sobering up. Some of the stages are sad, some are painful, some are angry, some are downright funny. I have not gone back to change what I wrote – I want you to understand that if you are going to start living sober your mind will also go through changes and stages.

The names of the people involved have been changed. I have tried to re-create scenes and conversations to the best of my memory. If I can't quote people verbatim, I hope you will at least be able to grasp the idea of what was said or done. This is told from my perspective, but I try to be extremely honest in my observations. My story, the people and activities I talk about are very personal. These are passed along not to glorify myself, it is done to document and better explain what being a drunk and sobering up is like. I relay my drinking history to you so you can understand what a large role drinking and getting drunk played in my life. I attempt to focus on my own errors and flaws as well as

11

some of my good qualities. I share stories of what transpired during my sobering up process – how I was berated and hurt by the person I trusted the most. I do this not to spew dirt and sour grapes, but I feel it is important to illustrate how the people that I counted on the most purposefully undermined me, and people that I least expected to care about me held my heart gently. I want you to understand that no matter what is done to you or said to you, no matter what collapses around you, no matter how useless your efforts appear, **you can stay sober**.

Your goal should be to get sober and stay sober while still enjoying a fulfilling and engaged life. You want to be able to go to parties, sporting events, concerts, etc. You want to be involved and participate in all the functions and activities you desire. You want to be fun to be around and you want to be around fun and constructive people. You can do all of this and have all of this – but only once you have accepted that sobriety is your own choice.

This book was not intended to be a literary masterpiece – it is far from that. It is written in a simple, crude and raw fashion. I wanted it to be easy to read, entertaining and helpful to people that want to live a normal life sober. My story is not glamorous - this is a story for the rest of us. This is a way to get sober and *stay sober* for the average person. It is a way to accept the real world with an open mind and live life to its fullest - SOBER. This has been a wild, volatile, crazy and painful journey for me, and it's nowhere near being over. I keep waiting for my journey to get to the end – but I guess that won't happen until I take my final breath – and sometimes it feels like that day can't come soon enough.

This can be the greatest achievement of your life. It may not be the most thrilling achievement, but in the end, it will be the best thing you ever did for yourself and for someone else.

Here is my ridiculous story.....

#1) How did this happen?

A look back at how I got started.

Can you imagine someone making this statement: "I know I'm just a little kid right now, but I can't wait until I get older and completely screw up my life with alcohol and drugs. I'll waste a lot of money; I'll sleep around and compromise my morals. I'll do all kinds of things that I'll regret, and I won't accomplish most of the things that I know I could or want to in life. I'll spend my time in college getting drunk – that's if I go to college – and I won't reach the level of education that I am capable of. I'll get fired from a lot of good jobs, get arrested, fail at wonderful relationships, ruin my health and hurt innocent people. I can't wait to get started!"

It's an old story, but it's true – no one ever plans on growing up to be a drunk or to have alcohol ruin their lives. No one in their right mind would ever plan for that, but it happens. Don't beat yourself up for it, don't hate yourself for it and don't let others make you feel guilty because of it. Just face the fact that it happened, you're now a drunk, alcohol controls you and you may think that you have possibly fucked up your life beyond the point of repair. But unless you're already dead, some things will be able to be repaired.

I never planned on alcohol controlling my life. I started drinking because it was "cool" – at least that's what my friends told me, and that's what the media told me. I'm not blaming my friends or the media. I became a drunk of my own free will. I grew up in Milwaukee, the beer capitol of the world. Drinking and getting drunk is part of the culture here. Festivals, bars, picnics, sporting events, even church festivals revolve around drinking beer. During the time that I was growing up, drinking was a huge part of our economy and lifestyle. Guys that worked at breweries were not only allowed to drink at work, they were encouraged. How cool is that? It was great to go on brewery tours here in Milwaukee. We would walk around the plant, listen to their bullshit about that brewery's history for an hour, then get tanked out of our skull afterwards. They would let us sit there and have as much free beer as we could drink after the tour. What a great marketing ploy. I would've never left except that the lounge closed at 8pm.

My parents didn't drink, so I was not raised in an alcoholic household. In fact, my dad's dad was an alcoholic and my parents steered clear of drinking. They didn't have a liquor cabinet in the house. My Dad kept his beer at the bottom of the basement stairs – a nice icy cold 54 degrees. A case of beer would last my parents six months or more. My mom and dad only drank on holidays, and if they did drink, it was no more than one or two cocktails. I can't remember ever seeing my parents drunk. My dad didn't come home from work and have a beer. There was no beer or wine with meals. My parents didn't try to keep us kids away from alcohol, it just wasn't a major part of their social life. I was the only one in our family to grow up and become an alcoholic. I did this all on my own.

When I was a kid of 6 or 7 years old, my aunts and uncles would let me have a drink of their beer. It didn't taste that great, and every time I took a drink of beer I would burp and it would fizzle up my esophagus and give me a burning sensation inside my nose. They would laugh at the goofy faces I would make, then they would offer me another swig. Thank God that I eventually learned how to belch properly. I'm certainly not blaming those people for me becoming an alcoholic. I became an alcoholic because of geo-psycho-social reasons. Geographically I lived in a community of drinkers. Psychologically I have a propensity to overdo anything. My social circle and career field glamorized drinking. Drinking became MY culture.

I still remember the first time I actually got drunk. I was 14 years old. I don't remember who got us the beer, probably one of my friend's older brothers. That's what older brothers are for, right? There were only about three or four of us and we got a case of Pabst Blue Ribbon, 24-12 ounce cans. It was January or February, and we went to the local public park and skated on the frozen pond. The city would clear off areas of the pond and we could skate there for free. There was a small building that we could change in and they had lockers for our shoes, etc. It was a weekend so my friends and I all went to Jackson Park to skate. Drinking beer and getting drunk was not in my plans, but one of my friends brought beer with him to the park. We took the case out on the island, shoved the cans in the snow and began drinking.

I never had more than a couple of sips from a beer before that. Shit, I was drunk after the first two beers. I still remember that after those first two or three beers it started tasting like water (does that sound familiar?) I stumbled around, fell over, laughed, got paranoid, laughed some more. I threw up in the snow at some point during the evening. Now for some people, getting sick and losing control of their thinking would make them not want to drink again, but not me. I was drawn to this euphoric sensation. Being drunk felt cool. I felt light, I felt alive, *it felt right*. I knew that this was something I was going to enjoy. Suddenly I couldn't wait until the next time I could get more beer.

We were all so young that none of us could buy beer, so we had to rely on older siblings. My brothers wouldn't buy beer for me. Can you believe that shit – my own brothers. It wasn't that they didn't love me or that they were worried about getting in trouble for buying me and my friends beer. No, they didn't want to do it because they knew it was wrong. Damn that moral upbringing by my parents! So we resorted to hanging around convenience stores and bars, asking younger looking strangers if they would buy us beer. Eventually somebody always did. I wonder how I would react if that would happen to *me* today?

I attended an all boys high school, and plenty of the juniors and seniors looked old enough to buy beer. Eighteen was the legal age at that time. I drank a lot in high school and didn't spend much time in class. I spent most of my days cruising around in cars with other punks and hoodlums. I would get to school in the morning, maybe attend a class or two, then meet up with my buddies. We'd go cruising and drinking, just hanging out around other high schools, causing trouble, getting into fights with other kids. Nothing really terrible, no felonies like robbery, mugging or burglary. High school was also when I learned how to enjoy smoking pot and the finer points of using many other drugs. Beer was actually my "gateway" drug. I was never interested in smoking pot until I started drinking.

So many people claim that pot is the gateway to drug use. I disagree with this. Beer, wine and liquor are so much more accessible and accepted in our society, that I believe most kids start drinking before they ever try illegal drugs. I'm not making a case for the prohibition of alcohol; I'm just sharing my own personal observation and experience.

I was never afraid of hard work and I always earned money, even when I was a kid. I had paper routes, mowed lawns, or shoveled snow. In high school I sold candy to pot-heads in my algebra class. At fifteen I started working at a gas station, pumping gas, doing oil changes, washing cars. I wasn't spending much time in school, so I worked a lot of hours. I eventually was put in the position to run the gas station. I handled the money, closed out the till, and kept the accounting records. I was honest too. I never stole from my employer. I was making good money and I had no interest in continuing my education. I had a gift for business – or maybe it was a gift for hustling?

My relationship with my parents during my early to mid-teens was explosive to put it mildly. I was a much bigger problem than my parents deserved. I was always getting into trouble. I would come home late, sneak out if I was grounded, get caught for smoking cigarettes, skipping out of school, fights at school, disrupting class, poor grades or being a punk with the staff – typical teen shit. And like a lot of kids, I thought it was fun to go to stores and shoplift. I stole useless crap, like rubber bands and gum. I only got caught once for shoplifting. My parents made me return a bunch of shit that I had stashed in my bedroom, even some of the crap I bought with my own money. I loved my mother but I would still be disrespectful. She would cry and pray the rosary for me – in Polish. (I can only guess that praying in some language other than English must have more influence with God.) I had many deep conversations with my mom. She tried her hardest to talk me out of being a punk. My mom kept a lot of things secret from our dad. She knew that he wouldn't be as understanding, compassionate and tolerant as she was. Dad wasn't violent, but he wouldn't stand for his kids not listening to him.

On the day I turned sixteen my dad took me for my driver's exam. I passed and got a temporary license. Two hours later I received my first speeding ticket. This was a sign of things to come. Within one month I received even more speeding tickets and my driver's license was suspended – but I still kept driving – I just didn't speed until I got my license back six months later. The day after my sixteenth birthday I left home.

I had my job at the gas station and my boss owned a motor home that he let me stay in. The gas station also sold used cars, and I had access to any of the cars on the lot that I wanted. I had it made. I would use one of the cars to go to school in the morning, come back and work in the afternoon until we closed at 8pm, then go out cruising at night, drinking beer. I'd pick up girls, bring them back to the gas station and go make out in the motor home. If a girl was extra adventuresome I would put a car up on the hydraulic lift and we would make out in the back seat.

I was just starting my senior year of high school and I attended for about a month until I decided that I was so damn smart that I

17

didn't need to finish high school. There was a school for "problem students" where I was allowed to go study for my G.E.D. The first day there I asked if I could start taking the series of (5) G.E.D. tests. I got a perfect score on the first – and only – test I took. The instructor couldn't understand why I wanted out of school. He tried with all his heart to convince me that I should to stay in school, graduate, go on to college and have a successful career in business. I was too smart for that shit. I never went back, never graduated from high school and I never received my G.E.D.

At sixteen I was a regular at a local tavern. Beer was ten cents a glass. Uncle Bert (not my actual uncle) was the bartender, and he was happy to serve me beer, even though he knew I wasn't old enough. In his mind: "at least this kid isn't out freebasing that marijuana stuff." At ten cents a glass a young kid could get pretty drunk. Uncle Bert was always half in the bag himself, so he'd just keep my glass filled and take a dollar for the night.

Drinking and driving wasn't a big deal during the 70's and 80's. If I got stopped by the police, they would usually just tell me to go home, sleep it off and don't do it again. They might call my parents, but normally I would just be sent on my way. My buddies and I would pile into a car I grabbed off the car lot, go out joyriding and drinking beer. Typically we would have at least a 12 pack for each of us in the car. Sometimes we would get into trouble – speeding, racing around, getting drunk and looking for fights. When you're a drunk young punk it's pretty easy to find someone to fight with you. We didn't commit crimes against innocent people; we always looked for other drunken punks.

I was always able to walk away from crimes like petty robbery or stealing stuff. I usually had drugs of some sort on me and I didn't want to get caught for something stupid like stealing tires, then get nailed for drugs. I also had some deeper morals. I didn't want to hurt innocent people and I never wanted to hurt girls.

During this time, I met the first real love of my life. Her name

18

was Gina and she was beautiful. I was a punk and she thought I was cool. Her dad owned a used car lot and I started working for him. Her parents let me stay at their house because I had nowhere else to stay. Gina's dad was a hardcore drunk and he and I got along marvelously. He taught me how to really drink. Not just beer, but vodka.

So imagine this: I'm seventeen, working 40-50 hours a week, being paid fairly well, staying for free at my girlfriend's parent's house, and as a bonus I get to bang my girlfriend whenever I want. I'm almost always drunk. I was wrecking cars on a regular basis. I would be drunk and drive off the road, smash into railings, get stuck in ditches, hit poles. I rolled an old Chevy pick-up onto its side coming into the driveway too fast one night. I thought that I was made of rubber and that I would never die.

I was picking up on all sorts of shady business skills while working at used car lots. I also learned a lot about cars, and I was becoming a damn good mechanic. I even started buying my own tools. I broke up with Gina – actually she dumped me – and I started working at Midas Muffler shops. I was making some real good money there. I taught myself how to weld and became a valued employee. I was starting to settle down a little bit and was becoming less of a hoodlum, but I was drinking even more. I was getting a little older, and I was developing a tolerance for alcohol.

I met my buddy Eric when I started working at Midas. Eric was a hardcore drinker too, so he and I hit it off right away. Eric and I would go out every night and get completely shit-faced stumbling drunk, but we always showed up for work the next day. Sometimes we smelled so strongly of booze from the night before that we had to stay out of breathing distance of people. The manager wouldn't let us talk to the customers; he would only let us work on their cars.

Bernie was the manager of the Midas shop and he was an ex-Navy guy. He would eat cigars! Not just chew on them, but eat the

19

fuckin' things! He never lit them, he just ate 'em. He was also a hard partying maniac, but he wouldn't tolerate any bullshit from his employees. He was strict. He didn't care what we did in our personal lives, but wouldn't accept anything less than perfect at work. He talked with me about the military and said that he thought I would make a fantastic soldier. I was tough, smart, had an attitude, didn't mind fighting or getting my ass beat, plus I was a hard drinker – all wonderful qualities for a serviceman.

One weekend I attended the Milwaukee Auto Show. There was an Army Recruiting booth there. I was drunk and thought it would be a brilliant idea to enlist, so I did. I figured that I would join the Army and be a mechanic. It sounded like a good idea at the time, so I signed a bunch of papers and was scheduled to go for a physical and enlistment exam. About a week later I showed up at the Army Recruiting center and started the process of enlistment. I passed my physical, and then took the written exam. After I took the exam I met with a recruiter. I explained that I wanted to be a mechanic. He looked at my test results, then he looked at me. He stared me right in the eyes and said, "What the fuck are you doing here?" I didn't understand what he meant. Then I found out that I had gotten a perfect score on my test. He picked up the phone and made a call. He then told me that I didn't belong in the Army, and he made an appointment for me with an Air Force recruiter.

The Air Force sounded even better, so I drove over to their recruitment office and started the process there. Almost the exact same thing happened with the Air Force recruiter. I passed my physical and took the entrance exam. I told the recruiter that I wanted to be a mechanic, and he said I would be better suited for the electronics field. Flying around in jets and fixing electronics on planes sounded pretty good to me, so I said "okay." Problem was, you have to have a high school diploma to join the Air Force. I told the recruiter that I didn't graduate and that I didn't even have my G.E.D. He pulled out my test results, looked at them, then looked at me and said, "Oh, you graduated all right, they must have lost your records."

At this stage in my life I had been drinking and smoking pot for almost four years. I had been living on my own for almost two years, and I had been running businesses or hustles for over three years. I was looking forward to traveling the country with the Air Force. I had no idea that I would also earn my wings as a professional drinker over the next two years.

#2) What a party!

How I kept it going without even trying.

Just like any dumb young guy, all I wanted to do was party and get laid and I probably could have gotten laid a lot more if I wouldn't have been so drunk all the time. I learned early in my drinking career how to deal with hangovers. During my late teens and early twenties it was fun to get really drunk and go to work the next day completely hung over – it was a challenge. I rose to that challenge and I functioned fairly well, even hung over as I was. I never had to have "hair of the dog" – you know, that drink first thing in the morning before work to get rid of the shakes. I actually liked being hung over. I knew that eventually, before I went to bed, I would be getting drunk again. As I got older I embraced drinking more and it became a major part of my life. Getting drunk became the focus and driving force of everything I did. **My entire world revolved around drinking.**

I thoroughly enjoyed my time in the Air Force. I liked the camaraderie of my fellow servicemen. It's an extraordinary feeling being part of a team that can kick the shit out of anybody or anything. My time in the service is where I learned the importance of personal responsibility and reliability. I learned how to accept orders and respect the hierarchy of authority. (I also learned how crucial it is to keep armpit hairs off my deodorant stick – I mean really, if I can't even keep pit hairs off my deodorant, how in the fuck can I be counted on to keep a missile silo clean?) But truthfully, the greatest thing I learned in the service was the power of self-discipline and how to use it as a winning tool in life.

However I didn't use self-discipline at that time to control my drinking. During that era, heavy drinking in the military was a badge of honor, and I earned plenty of merits and ribbons. Growing up in Milwaukee, I was trained early at how to guzzle. My fellow airmen were highly impressed at the amounts of beer and hard liquor I could consume.

My Air Force recruiter was certain that I would get an "Honor Student" ribbon during basic training. I didn't get the ribbon. I got one answer wrong on my final exam. After completing basic training at Lackland Air Force Base, San Antonio, TX. I was transferred to Keesler Air Force Base in Biloxi, MS. I ended up befriending and hanging with a group of guys that loved drinking and fighting. We would get drunk on weekends, spend all night on the beaches and get into a few fights. The best drunken fights happened when we would go to New Orleans.

I had come up with some bullshit story so I could go back to Wisconsin, pick up my car and return with it to Mississippi. I then became one of the few Airmen that had a car on base. My drinking buddies and I would pile into my car and drive to New Orleans, spend the weekend drinking and fighting. I would get so drunk that I can barely remember most of the shit we did. I am amazed at how drunk I would get and still be able to drive a car. We would usually get into trouble for getting back to base late on Sunday night or early Monday morning – still drunk, half bloody and quite often reeking of pot. All too often we would forget to dump out our dope, and I got busted a few times for that. The gate guards would normally throw out (keep?) our dope and then turn us in to our squadron commander. This resulted in weekend squadron duty or some other stupid punishment. It never stopped me from drinking or smoking dope. I scammed my way out of having to do my duty half the time by paying someone to fill in for me. I even led a charmed life in the military.

It was as if the military didn't really care about excessive drinking at that time. It almost seemed like it was a rite of passage.

Beer was dirt cheap on base ($1.25 for a 6-pack). All of my schooling, lodging, medical care and food was paid for, so I had plenty of money for beer and pot. The chow hall was open 24 hours, so we would go out and get shit-faced drunk, then go eat a ton of food. One particular night, my buddy Galen and I came back from a night of drinking and we went to the mess hall. It was about 2:00am and they were serving breakfast. It was cafeteria style, so you just walked down the line and grabbed what you wanted. I had heaped a bunch of food on my tray and at the end of the line stood the chef. He would cook you whatever kind of eggs you wanted: scrambled, fried, omelets. I'm all drunk and he asks me, "How do you want your eggs?" I said, "I don't care... fuck 'em up any old way." He leaned across the counter and slammed three raw eggs onto my food tray and said, "Here you go asshole." He showed me! I never said that again.

While I was stationed at Keesler AFB in Biloxi, I saw the greatest business idea ever – it was a place called *The Beer Barn*. It was a drive-thru bar. We would drive in, order a quart (or two or three) of tap beer and a bag of boiled crayfish or shrimp, then drive out! It was beautiful. It was legal to drink and drive in Mississippi (at least I think it was). I was in heaven.

After I was done with my aircraft training, I returned to Milwaukee and was on National Guard status. I was going to get a job in the electronics field, but I had a chance to go back and work as a manager of a Midas shop in Eau Claire, WI. I took that job because I learned that there were a couple of nursing schools in Eau Claire, and I was lookin' for pussy! I liked the Eau Claire area because it was not too overly populated and less than 100 miles from the Twin Cities. Eau Claire had a lot of college bars that I frequented. Once again, I was earning some pretty good money and I didn't lead a very lavish lifestyle.

I dated a lot of different women when I was living in Eau Claire. I would meet a new girl almost every night hanging out at the bars. These weren't all one-night-stands. I had a lot of very nice

25

girlfriends. I remember one woman in particular. Her name was Karen Fox, and was she ever a fox! What a sweet, wonderful woman. It was the way she handled herself, carried herself and treated me, that made me want to treat her like a REAL woman. I was too young and stupid to fully appreciate her at that time, but my relationship with her raised the level of how I treat and respect women today. She also taught me a lot about enjoying sex. I was a drunk young punk, but I knew good sex when I had it!

I drank every night after work while I was living in Eau Claire. I would head out to the bars and get completely loaded. I got pulled over a few times while driving home drunk. It's a small city and after the police questioned me and found out who I worked for they would let me go (another example of my good luck). The owner of the Midas shop didn't drink and he wasn't too fond of all the wild partying I was doing. I was a good employee. I did my job properly, represented Midas well and treated customers with respect. But due to my heavy drinking and punk-ass attitude, tensions began brewing between the owner and me. I didn't get fired, but I didn't feel like I was wanted. So I started making plans to head back to Milwaukee. Eventually I gave him my resignation – which he gladly accepted.

I left Eau Claire after about eight months. I figured I could go back and return working at a Midas Muffler shop in Milwaukee. Deep down inside I was hoping to hook back up with my old girlfriend, Gina. I was mixed up as to which direction I should go with my career. I was a good auto mechanic and I could easily get a job with Midas. I even had an executive from a new muffler chain call me and ask if I would be interested in managing a shop for them. It was called Meinickie but I would have to move to the Chicago area. Foolishly, I passed on this opportunity.

I had very good mechanical skills and electronics knowledge that I learned thanks to the Air Force. I ended up getting a job at a factory that built electrical smelting furnaces – those are giant machines that melt metal using electrical induction instead of gas or coal fired blast furnaces. This was during the time when Tylenol had their tampering incident (1983?), so this company also built assembly lines and machines that electronically melted the seal on top of plastic bottles. I was hired to work a second shift position. I got along great with all of my fellow employees. These guys were also hard drinkers. We would head out to our cars at lunch and sit there drinking beer and smoking pot for an hour. Our foreman was one of our fellow partiers, so he didn't care how drunk or stoned we got; as long as we got our work done before the shift was over. We did good work, but most of us were drunk. We got so bold that we would drink while we were working. There was a lot of smoke and welding going on inside the factory, so a couple of guys and I would smoke pot and do cocaine while we were working. (This is probably not what you wanted to hear about some of America's workforce – which is why companies do drug screening now).

Working second shift was perfect for me. I would be done with my shift at 11:00p.m. and I could go out to the bars after work. I didn't start until 3:00p.m., so I could sleep off all my booze and drugs from the night before. I started hanging out at some dance clubs and I got to know some DJs from a rock radio station in Milwaukee. I became friends with the morning show hosts. They thought I was pretty funny and they would let me do silly phone characters and goofy stuff for them on their radio show. They were very comfortable with me and I got to know a lot of other DJs. These guys started teaching me how to be a DJ and do radio production. I ended up becoming a fairly well-known character on radio. I started doing appearances for the radio station, and that's when my life completely changed. That's when the party really got cranked up.

#3) Drinking seemed pretty normal to me.

It was my way of life.

When I talk about the amounts of alcohol and drugs I consumed, I'm not doing it because I'm proud or that I want to be a blowhard. I tell you how much I consumed so that you get a reference point of what drinking and drugs meant to me. What was once a badge of honor for me is now just a sad statement of what I did with a lot of money and my life. I know that there are plenty of people that consume far more than I ever did. I refer to these quantities because it amazes me that I made it to the age I am. I should have either killed myself with alcohol poisoning, overdosed on drugs or died in car wrecks (hundreds of times).

Living my life drunk seemed pretty normal and natural to me. I never felt as if it was a problem. Oh sure, I was well aware that I would get *too drunk* on occasion, but what is *too drunk*? To me, too drunk meant that I felt like shit the next morning, that I had to drive home with one hand over my eye so I could see straight or that I woke up with a fat broad in my bed. I never got so drunk that I pooped myself, passed out in public or peed in bed. Okay, so I did pee in the hallway of a hotel in Vegas once, but I thought I was in the bathroom. I had gotten up in the middle of the night and thought I was walking to my bathroom – so I peed, woke up and found myself standing naked in the hallway – locked out of my room. In fact, I've woken up naked, locked outside of my hotel room a few times. I am told that I had attempted to pee in my dresser a few times as well, but my wife always stopped me before I could relieve myself in the sock drawer – I vaguely recall hearing "what the fuck are you doing?" So I guess I did get *too* drunk.

I have spent most of my adult life celebrating holidays, birthdays, vacations, any event – drunk. Every single occasion was structured and planned around drinking. Holidays were spent drinking a Bloody Mary early in the morning, followed by drinking the rest of the day. Without exaggeration, I would easily consume a minimum of a 12 pack of beer for any given holiday. If it was a summer holiday, say the 4th of July, that would be more like eighteen or more beers followed by half a bottle of Scotch. Birthdays, Thanksgiving, Christmas, Mothers Day, Fathers Day, Arbor Day, it didn't matter, I would drink all day long.

It wasn't any different if we were going out to an event. In those cases I would usually drink more. For example, if I was going with a group of friends to a Green Bay Packers football game, I would have a half gallon of Bloody Mary already pre-made. We would each drink a Bloody Mary before we hit the road. This would be either a double or triple shot, along with a beer chaser. We would then drink the Bloody Marys on the drive to Green Bay. This was about a 90 minute ride. Figure two each and smoke at least one joint on the way. Once we parked at the stadium, we started drinking beer. The cooler was filled, so I guess that I would drink at least six to eight beers before the game. While walking from the parking lot to the stadium we would each bring two beers – one for the walk, the other for standing in line to get in. Once we got in the stadium we would go straight to the beer concession for more beer. We wouldn't buy bottled beer – those were only 12 ounces – we would get tap beer because those were 24 ounces. I would drink four or five of those big beers during the game. All this beer created a lot of piss – hence I had to pee a lot. I spent most of the football game either standing in the beer line or standing in line to pee. If it was winter, we could sneak beer in under our jackets or I could bring in a flask filled with Scotch. After the game I would

30

drink one or two more beers while the parking lot emptied out and smoke another joint on the drive home. How I could still walk by the time I got home is beyond me.

Want to go golfing? That entailed a small thermos filled with pre-mixed Bloody Mary and a cooler strapped to my golf bag that held 10-12 beers. I would drink about six to eight of those beers and my golf partner would drink the others. If it was real warm out and we were in the mood to drink, we would finish the cooler full of beer and have the cart girl stop with beer a few times. We weren't just thirsty – we liked looking at her pink thong with the beads on it. (I always wondered how far those beads went?) After we were done with golf we would stop in at the clubhouse and share at least two pitchers of beer. A lot of times I would stop at a bar on the way home after golf, get a burger to eat and drink a couple more pitchers of beer. I would continue to drink beer the rest of the afternoon and evening once I got back home. When I reflect back I am stunned at how much beer I drank in a day, a week, a month, in my lifetime.

Being involved in radio and entertainment was a perfect match for me. I loved to drink, I liked doing drugs and I have no fear of making an ass out of myself in public – it seemed like fun work. Working in radio broadcast can be a very rewarding career field and it can be rather glamorous. As a radio host I got to meet a lot of celebrities, got to go to a lot of concerts, parties and public events. I was able to go behind the scenes and enter areas that the general public is never allowed access to. Radio hosts are the first level of celebrity. People can call me while I'm on-air, they can meet and touch me when I go out in public. You can't do this with TV or movie stars. Even the local TV anchorman is inaccessible, but a DJ can be touched. Depending on what format of radio you're involved in, being a party animal can be a benefit. I'm not saying that all DJs are drunks or drug addicts – far from it. Most are very well educated and spend a lot of time reading, doing research and furthering their skills and education. Many of them lead normal, sedate home lives. What I am saying is that

31

rock/rap/alternative radio broadcast is a great career field to get into if you like to drink and party.

I thought that being on the radio would be a great way to get my old girlfriend back. I figured that she would hear me, think I'm famous and want to start dating me again. Guess what? It worked! I ended up getting back together with her. Out of the blue she called me one afternoon – said she heard me on the radio and was wondering if I wanted to get together. We rekindled our relationship and it was going well for about six months. We had both matured (she more than me). She had developed into a stable young woman but I was still a drunken punk. I continued my drunken lifestyle and carousing. I was meeting a lot of other women through my career – my confidence was high – so I decided I would dump Gina this time (gee, ain't I cool?).

I dated a lot of different women during this period in my life. I am still proud of the way I treated women – even my one-night-stands. I always behaved as a gentleman and held women with respect and dignity. However, my drinking got in the way of my having some wonderful long-term relationships. I had a few regular girlfriends, but I really enjoyed going out and meeting new women. I wasn't always looking for sex, but I certainly wasn't going to turn it down.

Then I met Jessica (not her real name) – who would eventually become my wife of 23 years. I was completely blown away by her beauty, her charm, her wit and intelligence. I couldn't believe that she was even mildly interested in me. We must have dated almost ten times before we ever even kissed. She was without question the greatest thing to ever happen to me in my life. I will go into greater detail later about my relationship with Jessica.

For far too many years my life was all about drinking and doing drugs – mostly drinking. I would wake up in the morning, sit on the crapper and smoke a joint – the same way that other guys smoke a cigarette while sitting on the throne – then I would start my workday. I would spend the rest of my day smoking pot and wouldn't start drinking until early evening, unless it was a weekend or holiday – then I would drink all day long. The only time that I drank at work was when I was working at the electronics factory. I never drank at work when I was a DJ, but I sure would drink a lot after work.

So imagine this: I would get up at 3:30a.m. to go work as a morning show host. I would smoke a joint on my way to the local restaurant where I would have breakfast. I would read the paper and prepare for the show. After breakfast I would smoke another joint on my way to the radio station. I would get to the station before 5:00a.m. The show would start at 6:00a.m., so I would sit on the crapper and smoke a couple more bowls before going on the air. The sales people and management didn't get in until 8 or 8:30a.m., so I would go to the bathroom and smoke a little more dope during the long songs before everyone else got there. I was done with my air shift at 10:00a.m. Sometimes we would have a production meeting afterwards. Those would be done by about 11:00a.m. Then I would go to a local bar with my co-host or just drive around drinking. Hell, it was the end of my work day.

After my on-air shift I would try to nap for a couple of hours in the afternoon because I would either have a paid appearance to attend or I was going to go out partying. Paid appearances were great! They usually involved women, drugs and drinking. Typically I would have to be at a bar or nightclub and host contests or do something for the radio station. This was perfect work for me. Stand up in public, say something witty, get free drinks all night and get paid for it.

After I married Jessica in 1983 I began to settle down a bit. When I say "settle down," I mean that I wasn't participating in wild carousing and high-risk business activities. I kept drinking just as much – we were both drinkers – so getting drunk every night and driving while drunk seemed pretty normal to me.

33

I continued my career as an on-air radio personality for another ten years after I married. I am proud to say that during all those years I never deviated from my marriage vows. I went to most radio functions and appearances by myself and I always passed on opportunities to cheat. Eventually in 1993 my career as an on-air broadcaster came to an end. It may have been due to the consolidation of the industry, it may have been due to my unwillingness to move around the country, but it was most likely due to my excessive drinking. I must point out again that – at that time – I didn't think my drinking was a problem. I simply believed that my failures were due to bad luck. See, we drunks always like to blame someone or something else.

I met my best friend Mike in the spring of 1989. I was attending the wedding reception for a friend of my wife. Most of the people at this reception were horse fanatics – and I couldn't stand listening to people talk about horses anymore, so I went outside to smoke a cigar. I saw this big, tall, dumb-looking bald guy standing outside smoking a cigar too. I said what most guys say, "Hey, how ya' doin'?" Mike said, "I hate horses" and I replied, "I have a gun in my car." While we were comparing notes, we realized that our wives were already good friends and riding partners. This chance meeting developed into a wonderful couples friendship that lasted for more than fifteen years. Mike continues to be my friend to this day and he is an inspiration to me. I admire his high moral character, his intelligence and his brilliant sense of humor.

I love boating almost as much as I loved drinking and I spent most of my summers on the water. I would have to tow my boat to a local lake. I would drive to the lake, launch the boat and then get drunk. I would always drink a beer or two on the drive to the lake. Once I was on the water I would get good and drunk, then drive back home. I am truly amazed that I was never arrested or got in an accident. I remember backing my boat into the garage after a day out on the water – completely missed the open garage door and backed the boat into the side of the house! I was so trashed that I missed an open 2-½ car garage door. I ended up patching the hole I made in the siding with bondo – the shit you use to do body repairs on cars. I was such a royal fuck up – but I thought nothing of the incident

Jessica and I purchased a lake house in the spring of 1989. Owning a lake house was a dream come true for me, but lake living can be dangerous for a drunk. Now I didn't have to haul my boat to a lake – I could walk out my front door and hop right in my boat and start drinking. Guests would come over and what do you do? Fill the coolers with beer and go boating. Drinking and boating just seem to go together. I get along good with all of my neighbors and we would all party together. Most of them don't drink as much as I did, but drinking was second nature to all of us.

Here's an example of my lake life: I would wake up on a Saturday morning and see one of my neighbors working on his pier. I would go over to help and we would start drinking. One of our wives would bring out Bloody Marys and a couple of beers. Then we would keep working on projects and drink beer all day. Later, I would grill out and drink all night. One of us would start a bonfire and we would sit around the fire all night drinking. Mike and his wife would spend weekends with us. After hanging around the campfire our wives would go to bed, then Mike and I would go out on the boat and keep on drinking. We would be out on the boat until 2:00 or 3:00a.m. in the morning getting blasted. I'm surprised I could find my own pier some nights. We would just putter around on the water, drinking, talking, and listening to music. If we saw a campfire along the shore we would pull up to that person's house and crash their party – insult their friends and relatives, drink their beer and leave. My friends would joke around and call me "Captain Hazelwood" – in commemoration of the drunken boat captain that wrecked the Exxon Valdeez spilling two million gallons of oil into the Arctic Sea. In fact I named my first pontoon boat the S.S. Hazelwood. I never took risks on the water with other people on the boat, even drunk. Oh sure, I hit my pier a few times, ran into buoys and even drove into the side of another boat – that was docked at its own pier! Still, nobody was ever in danger while

35

on my boat. I always had plenty of life vests out and available and I made kids wear their life vests while on the boat.

Drinking is just so easy and convenient when you live on a lake and I'm sure that I was a bad influence on most of my neighbors when it came to drinking. Lake living is also very friendly. I would just walk across the yards to whoever was sitting out on their deck and start drinking with them. If I saw one of my neighbors outside, I'd grab a couple of beers and go hang out. Here're a couple of stories to show you how stupid I was.

My neighbor John is a hard drinker. He's a great guy and he would do anything to help me. However, I'm an idiot and when we would get really drunk I would challenge him to wrestle – usually in a mud puddle. The problem is that John is much bigger and stronger than me. He was also a S.W.A.T. officer and he served in Vietnam. This guy is trained to KILL people with his bare hands and I was dumb enough to wrestle with him. One night I just wouldn't quit – I wanted to keep on wrestling. Being the smartass that I am I kept egging him on. I'm so grateful that he didn't kill me. We wrestled and he pounded the shit out of me. I broke a couple of bones in my right foot and hyper-extended my knee backwards. I had to use crutches and then a cane to walk for the next six weeks. My wife made John sign an agreement that he would never let me wrestle with him again – I still have that signed agreement.

On another night, John and I went out drinking in an old military jeep. It was Memorial Day and he got to use the jeep because he was a member of the local V.F.W. Post. The jeep had a 50mm machine gun mounted in the back. It didn't work, but I wanted to play "Desert Rat." He drove down the road and I could barely hang on to the machinegun. John had to hold onto my pants to keep me from falling out. I cracked my head on something and I had blood all over my face. Then we went to the local bars along the lake and drank all night – I'm sure that I was a lovely (and entertaining) sight. Keep in mind that this jeep had been to Korea and Vietnam –

36

it had been through two wars – but we were so drunk that we got it stuck in a cornfield in Wisconsin. We ended up getting some guys from a bar to help us push it out. It's a small lake community and luckily John and I both new all the police, who took pity on us and gave us an escort home.

The great hotdog bun incident: All of our relatives would come and hang out at our place during the summer because we had a fun lake house. We would all go boating, swimming, play badminton, grill out, the kids could fish off the pier. It was a great vacation place for people. I couldn't have been too awful of a person – my in-laws always wanted to stay at our house when they came from out of town to visit. In this particular incident, my sister-in-law, her husband and their two boys (4 & 6 years old) were staying at our place for the 4th of July. All of us had been drinking, partying and boating all day. I don't remember this – but I am told – that I got up in the middle of the night, grabbed a hotdog bun and passed out naked in the middle of the kitchen floor. My young nephews found me during the middle of the night, laying there on the floor, still clutching a half-eaten hotdog bun in my hand – and I don't even like hotdogs. Supposedly this shattered them for life. (Just wait until they go to college – pass out drunk at a fraternity party and wake up with shaving cream in their pants, eyebrows shaved off and a carrot shoved up their butt – that'll really shatter them.)

I have been told that this incident was the last straw for my wife. She says that she lost all respect for me after this. In my mind it's not that terrible, but obviously it was to her. I could understand her being upset if I had done this in front of her grandparents, aunt and uncle or work colleagues. This was not one of the brightest moments in my life, but we were all drinking. I'm not excusing my behavior, I just don't see it as being that awful – I see it as being more of an embarrassment about myself. Yet it clearly hurt her and that was the start of the downturn in our marriage.

As that summer progressed I started drinking even more. Not only was I drinking about eighteen beers a night, I was pounding Scotch and Gin after the beer. It's hard for me to fathom how much money I wasted because of my drinking. In an upcoming chapter I will estimate how much I spent on beer and liquor – but I can't even start to total up how much stuff I broke, lost, damaged or bought when I was drunk. What a waste and what a fuck-up I was. I can only try to imagine how obnoxious and irritating I was while drunk. When I think about it, I don't blame my wife for leaving me, considering all my drunken bullshit she had to put up with. I wasn't physically abusive, but I'm sure I was extremely annoying. Getting that drunk seemed normal and natural to me. But I never had to deal with *me* as a drunk – I was me!

#4) I was a productive drunk.

Functionally drunk and proud of it.

I use this chapter to illustrate that there are plenty of fully functional drunks in this world. Functional drunks can have successful careers and be perceived as having a normal life, however behind the public scene there can be turmoil. This can include domestic problems, laziness, lack of closeness with partners and children, poor health and overall stress. I have learned that functional drunks miss out on many opportunities for a better life because they are too busy being drunk when no one is looking. There are many very successful professionals in this world that just happen to be drunks. That doesn't mean that they are bad people, it just means that they have a drinking problem. I believe there are a lot of other people who are hard working, dedicated, caring, helpful, smart and well educated that accomplish a lot in life – they just happen to be drunks. And many of these drunks I would be happy to do business with, spend time with, be friends with, and even have as a spouse.

This chapter may also sound self-serving, defensive, bitter, petty, egotistical, martyry etc. It's a short chapter so you can skip it if you wish. I feel it is fair game for me to talk about some of my accomplishments and what I put into my marriage. I think it is good for me to reflect on all of the positive things I did in my life and my marriage. Not so I can gloat, but to show that I have a good heart, that I loved my wife and lived with the best intentions. While it is true that I had a drinking problem, I was not the lazy, malingering, useless, pathetic drunk that my wife and her friends eventually portrayed me as being. I feel that this is an important part of my recovery process – self forgiveness – and it helps relieve some of my guilt. It also helps me solidify my resolve to lead a sober life, knowing that I am a valuable and productive person, capable of bringing good to others. I suggest you do the same – to reflect on the good that you have accomplished and brought to this world, even as a drunk.

I may have been a professional drunk, but I did lead an extremely productive life. I never directly got fired from a job for being drunk, never had family or friends disown me – even though my wife eventually left me. I didn't lose my house because I was a drunk – but my ex-wife took it (okay, she was entitled to it). I never killed anyone with my car, but I did get a drunk driving ticket and almost killed myself in a car accident because of my drinking. I can't remember how many other times I came close to killing myself while driving drunk. So not only was I a productive drunk, I was an extremely lucky drunk.

No matter what I was – or wasn't – doing for a job, I always found time and money to drink. That is why I say it all seemed pretty normal to me. One thing that I learned from working in radio is that; Perception = People's reality. I was – and still am – very good at projecting the *perception* that my life is wonderful and easy. However the *reality* is that my work is my life. I am the busiest unemployed guy that I know.

I have held numerous interesting jobs over the years. After working at a job for about six months or so I would get bored and move on to something else. I was always considered a good employee and most of my bosses were sorry to see me leave. Wherever I worked or whatever I did, I did it well. My fellow employees and bosses probably didn't know how heavy of a drinker I was. Only a couple people knew how drunk I would get.

My wife was one of them and I was the other.

I was not a complete and total fuck-up because of my drinking. I think my worst fault was that I became an underachiever due to my drinking. I had plenty of energy and drive. I made some of the best laid plans – but once I started drinking – all those plans would end up being put on the back burner. I can now see that I would purposefully devise projects to work on so that I wouldn't look like a lazy bum and a drunk. I did some of my best construction and home repairs while drunk. My neighbors are impressed by the beautiful block retaining wall that I built while I was completely gassed. The wall is straight, constructed to safe standards, glued together properly, back-filled with gravel and then covered with topsoil and sod. I have sided houses and garages, roofed buildings, built decks, done plumbing, you name it, all while drunk out of my skull. I lived a fairly productive life drunk.

I bounced around Milwaukee working at various radio stations, eventually opening my own business. I started an advertising agency specializing in comedic radio ads. I purchased tens of thousands of dollars in recording equipment and built my own recording studio. I recorded radio and television commercials. I produced comedy for hundreds of radio stations. I worked as an independent producer for some big name comedy syndicators. I even did comedy for ESPN Radio.

We bought our first house in 1985. I had some friends help me repair the inside drain tile in the basement. This was not a small project. It involved jackhammers, pitching the drain tile and digging big holes for sump pumps. This home repair would have normally cost $8,000 but I paid my friends with beer and pot. I put a new roof on the house, built a beautiful office and recording studio in the basement and did tens of thousands of dollars worth of home repairs myself. I did all of the regular maintenance on our cars for over 20 years, all of the oil changes and repairs. I installed new furnaces and central air conditioning in both of our houses. I reroofed both houses, put on new siding, and replaced all the windows. I remodeled our homes – which included redoing the electrical system and drywall work. I built piers, decks, did concrete work – the list could go on for pages. I estimate that I did well over $200,000 in remodeling, repairs and maintenance for us over a twenty year period. I lived by the axiom that "I have never been beaten by anything mechanical." Even after I was divorced, I would go over to my ex-wife's house and do home maintenance for her. I replaced a sump pump, put in a new toilet, fixed her furnace, replaced a water softener and more.

I am so good at mechanical projects that my friends and family consult me or ask me to do repairs and remodeling on their houses. My wife's friends benefited as well. I did home repairs, auto repairs, helped them with financial issues and did their taxes. One year, I prepared the taxes for one of her friends and I noticed that she had overpaid her taxes for the past three or four years. I spent hours preparing and submitting amended tax forms for her so she could get more than $1,400 back in overpaid taxes. She turned on me when I sobered up just like so many of my wife's other friends.

For over twenty years I got along marvelously with my in-laws (at least I think I did). They welcomed me into their family and accepted me as one of their own. My mother-in-law was always gracious around the holidays and would invite my family over for Thanksgiving dinner. My mother-in-law is a fabulous hostess and cook and would put on a delicious meal for everyone. Not only was I welcomed in, my family was as well.

My former father-in-law is a remarkable man. I treated him with the highest respect, not just because he was my father-in-law – or because he was a clergyman – I treated him that way because he is truly a kind and caring man. We became very good friends and I miss him dearly. For about ten years straight, I would take him to Las Vegas for his Christmas present. He may be a clergyman, but when we went to Las Vegas, we were just a couple of guys. We did a lot of bonding on those trips and we had a lot of fun together. I would get pretty drunk and he would put up with my stupidity.

We never did anything bad or anything inappropriate. But I have done a few things that I can be embarrassed about.

On one of those trips to Vegas I had gotten so drunk that the pit boss wanted to kick me out of the casino – and it takes a lot to get kicked out of a casino. I was a registered guest there, so instead the pit boss had security take me up to my room and positioned a security guard outside my room to make sure I stayed there. I guess I was being rude to some of the dealers, quoting lines from "Goodfellas," insulting them and their families. At one point I stood up at one of the Blackjack tables – with my right arm outstretched – and began singing "Deutschland Uber Alles" to one of the Russian dealers. Again, this was not one of my most shining moments.

I want to spend a little more time blowing my own horn (no one else will blow it for me). My wife was not aware of all the work I actually did (which she graciously admitted to me after we were divorced). She didn't realize how dedicated I had been to her over the years and how easy I tried to make our lives. I didn't hide things from her; I just figured that she didn't care how bills got paid or how things got fixed. I always wanted to spare her the details and complications of daily life – I was taking care of shit because I loved her. In hindsight I can see that was a big mistake on my part. She didn't know how much I actually did or how much money I saved us. I don't think she was cognizant of how good our life truly was (or how good I thought it was). I'm sure that she views it quite differently. Evidently our life *was* bad for her or she wouldn't have divorced me.

I must give my wife a lot of credit for making our life easy as well. She is not lazy – she did a lot of work around the house and never shied away from doing manual projects with me. She kept our house clean, decorated it nicely, is a fantastic hostess and bought a lot of furnishings for our houses.

While I took care of writing checks and paying all the bills, she

43

paid in her share to cover the monthly budget and I paid my half. I never stole from her or "lived off of her" as her friends claimed. We never got collection calls, never had our utilities turned off, we always had food, cars, and *stuff*. We lived what I would consider quite well for being middle-income class. She had the steady income working full-time while I pursued my radio career. My wife was the main "bread winner" of the family, but I always made a good income. This allowed me to be pretty generous for birthdays and Christmas. I enjoyed buying presents for my baby and I felt she deserved it – I wish I could have afforded even more. But no matter how much I did or how many gifts I gave her, I was still a drunk and more than likely very difficult to live with. I am so sorry for anything mean I ever said to her or anything bad I ever did. I am sorry that I never lived up to her dreams or expectations.

Even with all of my skills, I never reached the high level of success that I know I was capable of achieving, because I was always drunk. I would accomplish a lot of things, and do them all quite well, but drinking would eventually get in the way. I always thought that I never *made it* because of bad luck, but now I can see that it was because I was a drunk, and getting drunk was always more important to me. I can't solely blame alcohol for my inability to become as successful as I hoped I would, I am responsible for all of my own decisions.

I'm sure I could have plodded along through life in the same drunken way for many more years. Had I continued drinking, I'm certain that my wife and I would have grown further apart, eventually getting divorced anyway. I would have wasted more money, broken more things, failed at more career attempts and my health would have deteriorated. I also would have missed out on getting to know my dad, my sister, my brother, my friends and myself as well as I have.

#5) The wake-up calls that I slept through.

I just kept hitting the snooze button.

I am dumbfounded as to how much money this hobby has cost me over the years. It's sad for me to fathom the amount of money I spent on just booze itself. It's hard for me to put a finger on the price of everything, but I'll try to add it up. I have to take into consideration how much money I spent drinking at home – not only the booze and beer that I drank, but what I bought for my wife and to entertain my friends. Then add in what it costs to go out to a bar or nightclub and drink, then how many drinks did I buy for other people while out at bars? Then there's the food after bar time and all the other dumb shit I bought or gambled away while sitting in a bar. Let's not forget about going out to dinner, where drinks make up half or more of the bill. Now let's try to figure in the cost for all of the non-productive time spent with a hangover, or the poor work performed with a hangover, not to mention all of the things I broke, smashed, crashed or ruined while drunk. I can't forget to add in the car I totaled (more about this shortly), the higher auto insurance and D.W.I. tickets I had to pay for. God only knows how much my medical bills were. Lucky for me my insurance paid the hospital and the surgeon.

Just for the sake of simple math, let's figure out how much I spent on alcohol, using a very conservative figure of $10 a day. That's $3,650 a year, so over 30 years that comes to $109,500.

That figure would be the *minimum* cost of my alcoholism. I would estimate it to be closer to $250,000 or more. Not only did I foolishly spend money and lose money while I was drunk, my mind wasn't thinking clearly during the day while I was sober, so my financial judgment was not as good as it should have been. I'm not simply blaming the alcohol. Sometimes we make bad financial decisions because we make bad decisions. Booze is not to blame for every mistake – sometimes we're just stupid, at least I know I am. I must also be honest with myself and admit that I wouldn't have saved all the money I spent on alcohol or invested it wisely. I'm certain I would have wasted most of that money on something else anyway. But I'm also certain that I wouldn't have ended up with as much debt as I did.

It's extremely difficult to know how much money I spent and lost making poor purchases or financial moves over the years. But I can't look back and torture, berate or hate myself for it. It's done – the money is gone – I did what I did and now I have to work on being smart today and even smarter tomorrow.

The amount of money that I was spending should have been a wake-up call to me, but it wasn't. I also had family members telling me that for my own health and safety I should watch how much I was drinking. I didn't listen to any of those wake-up calls. I was in my early to mid 30's at this time. I was co-hosting a radio show on a rock station, so it was part of my job to make personal appearances at bars and events and drinking was all part of this. I drove drunk almost every night. I can't remember, but I don't believe my wife was asking me to slow down at that time. I know that she was worried about me, but I was invincible, so I wouldn't have listened to her anyway.

One night I finally accomplished the inevitable. I had been out at a concert with my drinking buddy Eric. We got completely hammered at the concert and hit a bar or two afterwards. Then I drove Eric home. I stopped in at his house to have *one more*. It was late and I was tired, so I slept for a bit on his sofa before I left. It was about 3:00a.m. As I was driving on the freeway heading home, I unconsciously decided to finish the nap I was taking earlier. But before I took my nap while driving, I set my cruise control at 70mph. The next thing I remember is a loud SMASH and an awful impact. Not just a bump, but a massive body crushing hit. I remember waking up at impact and looking out the front of my car. There was a cement wall right in front of me and I wasn't moving. I knew something was wrong but I didn't feel any pain (yet). My face and chest were wet and warm. I rubbed my hands on my chest and I started to freak out – my hands were covered with blood and it was gushing out of my face. I looked up at the windshield to check myself out in the rear view mirror. It was missing. The power of the impact knocked it off the windshield. I was lucky I couldn't see myself, I may have freaked out even more.

It's about 3:30 in the morning and no cars are on the road. I got out of my car and walked around to look it over. I couldn't tell if I was alive or if I was dead and looking at my own accident. I was covered with blood and it was running from my face all over my chest. I knew that I had to get to a hospital. I saw an exit sign for a street that I was familiar with. I knew that there was a gas station just off the freeway. I figured that if I could walk there they could call an ambulance for me (this was pre-cell phone era). I vaguely remember seeing a car or two driving past me on the freeway. I felt weak and figured that I would never be able to make it to the exit, so I started walking out in the middle of the freeway, hoping to flag down the next car that came by.

I wish I knew who stopped and saved my life, because the next thing I can remember is waking up in a bed at a hospital. I owe my life to whoever took me there. I can only imagine what kind of bloody mess I left in their car and how horrible I looked with my face all smashed up and bleeding. To this day I have never found out and I can't remember a thing between walking on the freeway and waking up in the hospital.

Lucky for me my wife worked at the hospital that I was taken to.

She is a highly respected nurse and they recognized my last name, so instead of just having an ER surgeon sew me back together, they called a specialist in plastic surgery. I had to lay there and wait about a half hour or so for him to arrive. I know that he wasn't too happy being woken up at 4:00a.m. and called in to sew some stupid drunk fucker back together.

I was so drunk – and he had no idea what other drugs I may have been on – that he didn't put me under. I didn't even get a local anesthetic; he just started working on me. That was extremely painful, but I figured I deserved it, so I just laid there and tried to endure it the best I could. I was very co-operative. He finally lightened up a bit but he didn't mince words while working on me. I got quite the lecture. He told me, "I'll do the best I can, but you sure fucked up your face." I was devastated. I was a fairly good looking young man, in fact many people actually considered me to be handsome, (and modest – let's not forget my modesty) but now I thought I would look like Frankenstein's monster.

Then to make matters worse, while I'm having surgery, a Sheriff Deputy comes in and asks me if I had been drinking. No shit I had been drinking – couldn't you smell it pouring out of me? Because my face was so fucked up they couldn't do a breathalyzer test, so they drew blood instead. Turns out I was .22 BAC (Blood Alcohol Content). For about a month after the accident all my friends called me "Mr. Baseball" because my face was all stitched up just like – you guessed it – a baseball. My face was all swollen, purple and bruised with two black eyes – I looked hideous. I can reflect back now and be grateful that my wife stuck by me. She supported me emotionally by telling me how much she loved me and how glad she was that I was still alive. She didn't criticize me or call me ugly. She had every right to dump me then, I looked terrible and she is a stunningly beautiful woman, but she stood by me. I owe her for that.

In any case, after I went to court and lost my license, I was able to get an occupational drivers license. That allowed me to drive 20 hours a week. It was kind of tough to do my job as a radio announcer with my mouth loaded with stitches inside and out. I couldn't speak clearly and I had problems enunciating words properly. Plus my face was all fucked-up looking, so how could I make public appearances? After I was convicted, I was required to attend "Drunk Driving School." The course was kind of interesting and only mildly thought provoking. Drunk driving school taught me how to not get caught for drinking and driving – but it didn't stop me from drinking or inspire me to quit. I have heard that same statement from other drunks who have been arrested and forced to attend drunk driving classes. I did slow my drinking down a little bit – but all dumb-dumb driving school did was teach me how to change my driving habits, not my drinking habits – I just didn't drink and drive anymore (or as much). Like I said, I slowed down for a while, but then I went right back at it just as hard and heavy as ever. In fact, the next ten years of my life are kind of a blur. How sad is that? Some of the best years and experiences of my life and I can hardly even remember them.

My car crash should have been my wake-up call, but all I did was hit the snooze button. I had plenty of wake-up calls before and after that event, I was just too stupid to pay attention to them. I'm sure that what I was experiencing was simply denial. I knew I drank too much, I guess I just didn't want to admit it to myself – what drunk does? Even though I was well aware that I drank a lot, I thought that I had "it" and myself under control, but getting drunk was an uncontrollable part of my life. I was proud of how much beer and liquor I could consume. Like any typical bone-headed macho guy, I thought that hard drinking was a badge of honor. Pounding down twelve or more beers at one sitting was commonplace for me.

My heaviest drinking occurred during the summer months. My main goal was to get completely blasted every day. And every summer I would do at least two or three stupid, costly things – not to mention the embarrassing, humiliating and relationship damaging things I would do. I feel that I'm a fairly smart guy but I would do totally stupid shit. Break, smash, crash or lose things, wake up the next morning and feel bad about it, then do it all over again the next night. Why? Why couldn't I figure it out? Oh yeah, I forgot, I was addicted to alcohol, I had no respect for my own willpower and I was a stupid fucker when drunk.

Every summer I would cause at least $300 to $500 damage to my boat. Break a propeller blade, bang into the pier and bend the trim on the boat. Take off without pulling up the anchor, run over buoys. It would have cost me double or triple that, but I was capable of doing my own repairs. I would also typically injure myself at least two times during the summer while drunk – slipping off my boat while covering it, falling down a hill, walking into something, or getting hurt while wrestling with my neighbor.

My wife would have a talk with me about once a month regarding my drinking during the summer. It would be a civil, helpful talk, asking me to "please control my drinking." Or she would leave me a loving, tender note after a night of my heavy, belligerent drinking. Every note or talking to that I received was pleasant and based on concern for me, my health and my safety. Why didn't I listen? Why didn't I wake up before it turned out to be too late?

For your own sake, please don't do what I did. Listen, pay attention, and hear the wake-up calls. Don't hide from them; all you're doing is bullshitting yourself. It took me almost 12 more years of drinking and ruining more things in my life before I finally heard my final wake-up call.

#6) The wake-up call I finally heard.

What a rude awakening.

I can still remember the night I finally realized that I had to stop drinking (I'll expand more on that night in Chapter 7). Prior to that awakening, I had gone through a period that lasted about two years where I would consider quitting, but I kept putting it off. I kept thinking that I had my drinking under control and all I needed to do was drink just a little less – and like any good drunk – I would say, "I'll do that tomorrow, or at least by next week sometime." As I've mentioned, my doctor would remind me on a regular basis that I should quit drinking, not just control my drinking, but QUIT drinking altogether. I have very high blood pressure and he felt that my heavy drinking was one of the causes. Oddly enough, even after I quit drinking my blood pressure hasn't changed. A few people think I also still have some anger and bitterness issues – which I'm sure I do – but I'm okay with that.

It is often said that you have to hit bottom before you quit. Every day there were signs, the wake-up calls. Every day I would get closer to my bottom. There was no single occurrence that awakened me; instead it was a series of events. I kept hearing three distinctly different wake-up calls. The first call was that I was afraid that I would lose my wife. Even with the problems that we were having I never wanted to lose her. The second was that I was afraid that my wife would lose me. I was drunk and stupid and I wasn't thinking clearly about my relationship with her and I was afraid that I would stray from her. The final sign – I was afraid that I was losing myself. I no longer had control over my life or control over how much I was drinking.

The following story is heart-wrenching for me to write about. It is painful and embarrassing. I cannot hide from the facts of what I have done. Hiding from truths is one of the reasons I drank. I want to share this with you to illustrate that we all make mistakes in life, drunk and sober, but we can learn from our mistakes and we can make permanent changes within ourselves. I must accept responsibility for my own actions and accept the consequences.

This is was loudest, blood curdling wake-up call I got. I talked myself into compromising my own morals and my vows – I feel that this is the worst thing I have ever done in my life. But at the time, I felt as if my wife had abandoned me, that she was neglecting me. Her horse, her horse friends, her horse hobby and alcohol were all more important to her than I was or our marriage was. These conditions turned out to be true and may be considered mitigating circumstances that contributed to me compromising my marriage vows – however I am the only one responsible for my actions. No one forced me. Regardless of whether any of my friends feel that some of my actions were justifiable, I ultimately must accept ownership for anything that I have ever done. I was a bad husband. I allowed myself to think that another woman would solve my problems. How strange that my own wife who claimed I drank too much wouldn't help or support me to become sober. Another woman would be the catalyst to getting me to realize that I HAD to sober up. I never planned on having an affair. I never dreamed of other women and I didn't fantasize about other women when I was making love to Jessica. She was all I ever wanted, I married my dream come true. But tensions were building between us. She was neglecting me more and more. Her horse hobby and horse lifestyle were clearly becoming more important to her than our relationship.

I must protect the innocent, but I need to use a name, so for the sake of simplicity, from here on out I will refer to the other woman as **Lorna**. Here's the story of how I met the woman that changed my life forever.

The four of us, Jessica, Mike and his wife Sandy went on a trip to Las Vegas. It was Easter vacation, late March 2005. This was going to be a Birthday/Anniversary combo trip. We were celebrating Mike's and Jessica's birthdays, along with it being my 22nd wedding anniversary. The tension and uneasiness was beginning to boil within both of our marriages. Mike and I felt like we were being neglected and abandoned for the girls' horse hobby. We thought this trip would be good for us to all hang out without any horse distractions and that it would be just a normal trip. We had a few sightseeing events planned; Sandy had never been to Hoover Dam. We talked about all four of us going to a strip club, Caesar's Palace for dinner, hanging out together, gambling.

The trip started off on a bad note. Sandy & Jessica got hammered on the flight out to Vegas. They had filled up a water bottle with vodka, which at the time I thought was plain water. I just thought they were goofy, giddy, acting wild, but just having fun. We landed in Vegas, got the car and dropped off all of our luggage at the Golden Nugget, then hit the liquor store. We loaded up on beer, wine, Champagne and vodka, then we headed out to Hoover Dam. We stopped at the Lake Mead marina for lunch. The girls were drinking from the water bottle all the way there. The bottle had been refilled with vodka. We had lunch and they continued to drink. Then we drank more at Hoover Dam. That's when I figured out that they had been guzzling vodka all day. The girls were wild, shitty and belligerent towards us. I'm not claiming that I was a perfect travel partner. Hell I was getting mad and I was getting shitty with them. Luckily the girls passed out in the car on the drive back to the hotel.

That first night we went out to dinner together. Sandy got all pissed off because the waitress hadn't come and taken our drink order fast enough, so she got up and stormed out of the restaurant. The three of us stayed and had dinner. We walked back to our casino and started our night of gambling. Sandy was still pissed off, she and Jessica got wild, loud and drunk. By 8:00p.m. they were so loud and drunk that the "pit bosses" were standing by our blackjack table and asking them to keep it down. By 8:30p.m. my wife was so drunk that I had to walk her back to our hotel and pour her into bed. Remember, I was drunk too, but I was a professional drunk. I would pace myself. I'm sure that as far as my wife was concerned, I wasn't pleasant to be around. I was no doubt an argumentative asshole.

I returned to the casino for a night of gambling and drinking. Mike and I hung out for a few more hours. Mike was tired so he headed to his room around 11:00p.m. I would typically stay up all night gambling and drinking, and that's exactly what I did. I was sitting at a blackjack table when a beautiful young woman sat down next to me and started playing. I'm a friendly, harmless guy, so I talked with her at the table while we played. I'm a good blackjack player – even while I am drunk – and she was asking me for gambling advice. We talked about all sorts of things – just normal conversation. She told me about her job, why she was in Vegas, and how she had just gotten a "boob job". She was very proud of them (her new boobs). I complimented her (and her new boobs) but I remained a gentlemen. She asked if I was married and where my wife was. I didn't speak ill of Jessica, I just said she was up in the room sleeping. I mentioned numerous times that I was a married man – married to a stunning woman for 22 years.

Lorna continued to flirt and engage me in conversation. I was evasive with my answers to her personal questions. She was smart, gorgeous and compelling to speak with. We played blackjack, talked and drank until about 4:00a.m. She said it was time for her to head to her hotel. Turned out she was staying at the same hotel I was, and in the same tower. I was on the 14th floor and she was on the 12th. I walked her back to the hotel. I held doors open for her, spoke pleasantly, and was courteous. I saw her to her hotel room, I told her that it was a pleasure meeting her, and then I left and went to my own room. As I said earlier, I was a perfect gentleman and did nothing inappropriate. Even as a married man, I did nothing that anyone would consider inappropriate.

The next day at the pool we were all sitting around drinking and talking. "So what did you do last night Mark? Did you make any money?" I told everyone the story, "I made a couple of bucks. I met some woman. She's a lawyer in Seattle or somewhere, she just got new boobs, she was very proud of them. So, where are we going for lunch?" I didn't even remember this woman's name. I had absolutely no interest in this person at all. I could talk so openly about what I had done the night before because that's the type of marriage I had. My wife knew she could trust me implicitly and that if I was paying attention to another woman it was only out of courtesy or because I was being polite. I had always been faithful – my wife could count on me for that. Even though we were having a tenuous time, I was a married man. That is something I never forgot. I had always respected my marriage vows.

That afternoon we sat around the pool guzzling beer, wine, and mixed drinks. We eventually ate and headed out for a night of gambling. The same thing happened again that night – the girls got drunk, wild and loud. Once again I ended up walking them both back to the Golden Nugget by 8:00p.m. I returned to the Las Vegas Club to gamble and drink. Next thing I know, this woman from the night before is sitting beside me again. I was half in the bag and had an attitude because I was mad at my wife. I was a total smart ass towards this woman. I had absolutely no interest in pursuing her – I was married. She tried to engage me in conversation but I was being very cocky. She got irritated with me and got up and left. It made no difference to me. I was too busy getting drunk and feeling pissed at my wife.

As I walked around the blackjack tables I saw her again. I went over by her and with my best "puppy dog" eyes said I was sorry

55

and that I hadn't meant to irritate her. She invited me to sit down and play cards next to her. She had a very sharp wit and was very smart. She said "You don't even remember my name, do you?" I had to admit that I didn't. She took out a business card and circled her name. "Now remember it," and handed me her card. I can only guess that because I was acting disinterested she was drawn to me even more. Mike saw how she was acting towards me and he walked right up to me and said, "This is dangerous, this ain't good Mark, be careful." There wasn't any doubt in my mind that I was safe. What was I going to do? My wife is in our room, (drunk and passed out) but I'm married and completely faithful. I was so overconfident with myself that I hung out with Lorna all night, drinking, playing cards, flirting, drinking more. Mike warned me a couple more times – he told me to be careful. I reassured him that I was safe.

We played cards for a few more hours. Then Lorna wanted to go sit and talk privately. I figured why not – I'm drunk and pissed at my wife – besides, how much trouble could I possibly get into? I was enjoying her company and the flirting. It felt wonderful to have a beautiful woman showing interest in me again. I knew that I was playing with fire, but I had no reason to question my dedication to Jessica. While we were sitting playing some video poker in a quiet corner of the casino, Lorna moved closer to me. Her hair was up in a bun and she let it down and shook it out like a Miss Clairol commercial. She went from a professional sexy looking woman to a long haired SEXY looking woman. She slowly leaned into me, looked me in the eyes and asked me to kiss her. I was a bit surprised, but I figured sure, why not, what's one little harmless kiss? I gave her the kind of kiss that you give your Aunt when she knits you something nice for Christmas. She wasn't impressed. She said her grandma kissed with more passion. She wanted to know what it was like to be really kissed by me. That's when I gave her a kiss! A kiss like a *man* gives a kiss.

By this time I'm fairly drunk, but because I'm a professional drunk, I'm not sloppy, slurring or stumbling. I can walk, talk and act quite charming – I just happen to not be able to think too soundly. We walked back to the Golden Nugget and I escorted her to her room. She invites me in. Since I'm drunk and stupid, I accept the invitation. I'm a bit nervous, but I know I'm safe. I wasn't expecting anything to happen and I felt that I could handle anything that would possibly tempt me. I had no intentions of making out, having sex, nothing. I thought we would talk a little, flirt a bit more, then I would be on my way back to my room.

Lorna said that she had to go to the bathroom and asked to be excused. "No problem, I'll just stand here and drink my beer." A few moments later she comes walking out of the bathroom, NAKED. Holy shit! I wasn't expecting this. She approaches me, we hug, we kiss, I caress her breasts. We fall to the bed and continue making out. I freak out. What the fuck am I doing? I'm married, I'm married! Get out of here – you can't do this Mark. Tell her you can't do this. Leave, run, go, now! I gotta go, this is nuts.

There's too much shit going through my mind. I can't believe where I am and what I'm doing. I had never done anything like this before. I am attracted to Lorna but I am reeling with guilt. I'm drunk, can't think straight and I'm saying, "You're a beautiful woman. I'm married, you're married, we can't. Holy shit, I'd love to, but I can't, I, I, I gotta go." Lorna keeps telling me to keep my voice down so her work colleagues in the next room won't hear me. She's worried about getting caught. We kiss for a final time and I leave.

I get back to my room. I feel terrified and guilty. I can't believe what I had just done and I can't sleep. I have to be up in two hours to leave for the airport. What the fuck did I just do? I was numb and in shock on the flight home. I was dying inside. I wanted to tell my wife what I had done and ask for her forgiveness. I was freaked out. Everything changed; my head, my heart, my soul and my life were never the same after that.

57

When I returned from Vegas I didn't plan on pursuing any communication with Lorna. This was something that I needed to forget about and get over, but I have to admit that I kept thinking about her – probably because she had paid attention to me. Now that we were back home, Jessica and I continued on with our volatile relationship. I was drinking even more and acting even cockier – now that I had the reassurance that women were still attracted to me.

Lorna and I had exchanged email addresses but I didn't try to contact her – I knew that I had to leave this alone. A few days passed when I unexpectedly got an email from her. Before I knew it we were emailing each other every day. Within a couple of weeks we were emailing a few times a day, then live chat, then phone calls. Most of the emails and phone conversations were about normal, everyday topics. We talked about our jobs, our pasts, our individual goals. We discussed philosophy, talked about her kids and their hobbies, how they were doing in school. She worked at a prestigious law firm. She was very smart, well educated, a creative thinker and speaker, plus she was very sexually appealing. She would invite me to talk in a sexually spirited tone. She didn't want me to "talk dirty," but she did enjoy my wry sexual wit and double-entendre. We figuratively cried our personal and marital woes on one another's shoulders.

This was one of those turning points in life, the proverbial fork in the road where six months later you say, "What the fuck was I thinking?" It's usually about six months later when you can review what has transpired and look back at your behavior and see the error of your ways. So often we make big mistakes in our lives – usually while we are drunk. We do things that make sense at the time, but turn out bad later on for us and for others. We end up looking at ourselves in the mirror asking, "Why was I so stupid? How could I have done that? Why couldn't I see that this was such a bad move?" Non-drinkers do these things too, but we drunks have a propensity for making ill-thought-out decisions and this was another one of mine. No matter how I try to rationalize it out, my actions were not justified. I'm sure plenty of you might be thinking, "That's all you did? That ain't shit compared to what I've done."

I began drinking even heavier and my sense of reality was skewed. I wasn't thinking based on facts or truths, I was delusional and drunk. I was communicating more frequently and intimately with Lorna, but I knew deep down inside that it wasn't right for many reasons. First it wasn't right to do to my wife. I had taken vows and I had given her my word that I would be faithful. I knew what I was doing to Lorna's life was wrong. She was married and had two children. Her husband had no idea what was going on. He was oblivious as to why his wife was unhappy with him. I wouldn't have wanted somebody to do that to me, so I couldn't do it to somebody else. I couldn't ruin some other man's life and marriage. I didn't know this guy but I knew that his wife was unhappy and she was attracted to me. She was willing to end her marriage so we could start a life together.

I sat and got drunk at night and thought about this. How could I possibly fuck up the lives of so many people? How could I do this? I estimated that if I pursued this affair and we both ended up divorced and remarrying one another, I would have personally fucked up the lives' of at least 50 innocent people – her kid's, her husband's, my wife's. I would have drawn our friends and families into this mire of crap.

Lorna wasn't hostile in the way she talked about my wife, but she didn't try to talk me into working out my marital problems either. Why would she? We were having an internet/phone affair. I didn't speak poorly about her husband or try to pull her away from him. Instead I would often ask if she had tried to tell her husband how she felt and if she had spent the time to let him know what would make her happy. She would tell me how she had talked with him "a hundred times, but he just won't listen, he doesn't care, he's stubborn." I had every opportunity to badmouth this guy, but I didn't. Maybe that's what made me seem even more attractive to her? I believe that Lorna wanted me to divorce my wife and charm her into divorcing her husband so we could get together. Ahhh, the sad story of what happens when two married people that feel neglected find each other.

Regardless of how I try to spin this and make myself look like a nice guy, I understand that what I was doing was inappropriate.

This wasn't a torrid, sex-laden affair. It was an emotional and intellectual internet/phone affair. We didn't web cam each other, no cyber sex, no naked pictures, or any other pictures for that matter. We exchanged books and music CDs. She wanted me to hear her favorite country songs and I wanted to expand her tastes into rock. I was paying more attention to my communications with Lorna than I was to my own wife. I felt my actions were justified because I thought that I was being abandoned, while my wife was pursuing her horse riding hobby more obsessively. This led to us arguing more, which then led to both of us drinking more and spending less time together at home. That resulted in less time entertaining our friends and enjoying our lake house.

I had a younger woman paying more and more attention to me while my wife was paying less and less attention to me. My wife became meaner and drunker, and so did I. I began to think about taking this long distance internet/telephone affair to the next stage. I had an infatuation for Lorna – I felt a false sense of love. In my drunken state of over-confidence, I believed that I had someone waiting for me in the wings if I wanted. I was angry at my wife – I thought that I could leave my wife and this other woman could step in without ever missing a beat. Oddly enough, it was "the other woman" that made me wake up and realize that I needed to sober up and pay attention to my wife. I have heard that an affair can scare someone back into the arms of their spouse. That is exactly what happened to me.

While this internet affair of mine was going on I was drinking about 30 beers a day, then drinking Scotch at night after the beer.

That is when I woke up and realized I needed to pay attention to what was happening in my life. I had tried talking with my wife during the day while I was sober, but I didn't do it in the way she wanted to be approached. I'm sure that I would argue and say things in sarcastic ways. At the time, I was communicating the best I knew how. I told her that she was drinking too much and spending too much time with her horse hobby. I wasn't much better, I was still drinking heavily. I said that this wasn't healthy for our marriage and I asked that we go to marriage counseling. She didn't want to hear what I had to say. She thought I was just mad about her horse, that I wanted to control her and that I didn't want her to have any fun. We would both get drunk every night – and not always together. I would get mad that I was being put into 3rd, 4th or 5th place in the order of importance in her life. I remember that we would argue almost every night in the kitchen. One night I wrote out a list of what was important to her:

#1 her horse
#2 her horse friends
#3 wine
#4 her job
#5 me

She would tell me that I was jealous, or that I was a jerk because I wouldn't support her horse hobby, I was controlling or that I just didn't want her to have any fun. There was plenty of mutual name calling and plenty of arguments. These arguments would get pretty loud and heated but no worse than any other married couple. I never got violent. She didn't hit me or throw things at me. We would yell and get pretty upset with one another, but nothing was ever said that couldn't be forgiven. (I am telling you this story from my perspective. I must once again admit that I would get pretty drunk and I'm sure I was an asshole, so maybe I did say things that couldn't be forgiven.) We would typically go to bed angry, but we would both get over it the next day, or the next time that we made love.

My wife would go off riding her horse and I would go golfing and then boating. I'd get drunk and she would come home drunk. Typically she would bring home one or two of her horse riding girlfriends and they would continue to drink wine either in the kitchen or on the deck. Rarely would they get home early enough to go out boating before it got dark. After Jessica would head off to bed, I would sit in the living room, drunk, staring at the wall. I would try to understand and make sense of all this. I tried to get a grasp of what was all taking place around me. I realized that so much of this was my own fault, but I wasn't sure what to do about it. When I got more concerned or confused, I just had another beer. Drinking was always my answer, but I knew it wasn't the right answer. That's when I realized that we had to look for outside help and I came to the conclusion that we needed to see a marriage counselor. That is also when I knew my play affair with Lorna had to come to an end.

My wife was in no hurry to go to marriage counseling. She kept putting it off until I finally insisted that we go. Our relationship was extremely explosive by that time. One day she would be nice to me, the next day she would be pissed. One day I would be nice to her, and the next day I would be a jerk. This was no way to live. I had never been this confused about my marriage. I didn't know what was happening, but I knew I had to change something.

I had the luck to have the right person tell me at the right time that I needed to quit drinking. It only took a few moments and I made the decision to quit drinking. This person didn't say many words, didn't threaten me or didn't even try to persuade me with logic. He was our marriage counselor and all he said to me was this:

"You two don't have a marital problem, you two have an alcohol problem! Are you willing to go into treatment?" I followed up with, "What time do you want me there?"

I was more than willing. I was willing to try anything to salvage my marriage. I didn't realize at that time how damaged my marriage was or how difficult and tumultuous my life was going to get. I couldn't imagine that the one thing I should do to salvage my marriage – quit drinking – would actually play a role in ending my marriage. I was a drunk and I decided to quit. My wife was drinking heavily as well but she decided to keep on drinking.

My life changed at that marriage counseling session. I have not had another drink since (10/12/05). I immediately began addressing the flaws my wife claimed I had. I became more responsible, I was trying to mold myself into the man that she wanted me to be. I got the kind of regular job that she wanted me to have. I was earning a fairly decent income and I had quit drinking. Despite all of those changes I still lost my wife. I also ended up without Lorna. Everything played out just how I imagined it would on those drunken, lonely nights staring at my living room wall. I ended up divorced, broke, alone, no retirement, no health insurance, depressed and suicidal. But you know what? I'm still glad that I sobered up.

My affair died a slow natural death. Lorna didn't know it was dying. She would call me occasionally. She would still email me on a regular basis. After my divorce was final, she invited me to come visit her. I knew this wouldn't just be a friendly "how ya doing" kind of visit. She wanted to rekindle this affair if not take it a step further, or at least fuck me frazzled. I asked Mike what he thought I should do. He said, "If she is still married or even if she is only separated, it isn't right for you to do it." How about that? My friend has morals. I made the right decision – I didn't go. That was one of those turning points in life, that fork in the road where I went in the right direction. Too bad that when you make the right decision you don't get the same obvious results as when you make the wrong decisions.

I just stopped responding to Lorna's calls and emails. I'm sure that Lorna didn't have any intentions of finding a new man when she went to Las Vegas. I was not on her list of "things to do today." I'm certain I screwed up her life just as badly as I screwed up mine. I was drunk when it all started and I was drunk and delusional while this was all going on. But no matter how drunk I was I cannot blame alcohol for my actions, I can only blame myself for getting involved in that situation. Lorna is no longer part of my life. In the end, I guess I got what I deserved.

#7) Where is your bottom?

Mine was right in front of me.

People around you may think you keep hitting bottom, but we drunks can't see it until we're goddamned good and ready. An outsider looking at my life would have said numerous times over the years, "He finally hit bottom this time," – but I never did, I always came back for more. Most people would think that I would have hit my bottom when I almost killed myself in a car accident, or when I lost my driver's license, or when I came close to being arrested a second time less than a month after my accident, or when I drove my boat into another boat that was tied up to its own pier. Nope, I never saw those things as my bottom. As I said earlier there was no single event or occurrence that happened to me that gave me my big wake-up call. My wake-up call finally came when I experienced a series of events that were due to my drinking and even after my final wake-up call, it took me about two more months to take action and stop drinking. I wanted to keep hiding from reality.

I could see every aspect of my life spiraling out of control. I wasn't living up to the standards I knew that I was capable of. I wasn't working as well as I could. I wasn't paying attention to my marriage. In the deepest private corners of my mind, I knew that everything was falling apart because of how much I was drinking. But once I would start drinking for the day, *I would just fade off into a busy drunkenness.* (Does that statement ring true for you as well?) I was always busy doing something, trying to make myself look and feel productive. I would create an atmosphere of being busy. I would tell myself, "I'm too busy doing so many things that I don't have time to focus on my problems." But I always had time to drink. I would blame my failures on bad luck, not enough time, too many responsibilities, nobody helping me, etc. All of these excuses sounded valid to me when I was drunk.

I knew something wasn't right with my life and I figured that it had to do with my drinking, but I didn't want to face the reality that I was responsible for my own problems. I wasn't consciously searching for a life altering epiphany, I wasn't expecting that I would suddenly see that I had hit bottom. I feel extremely fortunate that I finally saw my life falling apart, but once I did see it clearly, some things were too far gone to repair and salvage. **I hit bottom too late** and some great things are lost and gone forever from my life. Following is the story of when I *unexpectedly* saw that I had hit my bottom:

I remember that I was sitting in my living room, about 1:00a.m. listening to loud music, staring at the wall, drunk (again). I wasn't sloppy shit-faced drunk, I had my typical nightly buzz going. I sat and stared at the wall, and for the first time I visualized what my life would be like without my wife. I sat there and I thought. I stared at the wall. My stomach began to roil into knots, I began sweating, I became nauseous, my heart pounded faster and faster. I could feel my throat constricting and I was feeling as if I was going to puke. I was shaking and terrified. I couldn't imagine living without Jessica in my life. I felt horrific fear and I sensed the reality of what I would lose if I kept drinking. (I already stated these in chapter 6, but I believe they are worth repeating). #1 - I was afraid that I would lose my wife. Even with the problems that we were having I never wanted to lose her. #2 - I was afraid that my wife would lose me. I was drunk and stupid and I wasn't thinking clearly about my relationship with her and I was afraid that I would compromise my integrity and stray from her (which I was already in the midst of doing). #3 - I was afraid that I was losing myself. I no longer had control over my own life or control over how much I was drinking.

I had no single catastrophic event take place; instead I finally saw and felt reality unfolding before me. I had seen reality before, but this time I truly accepted it. **That's when I hit my bottom.**

I didn't stop drinking the second that I had consciously hit my bottom, but I knew that I had to stop. It would take another 2 months of curtailing my drinking, feeling guilt and painful mental turmoil before the day came that I actually stopped drinking forever. I had my last drink the day before my first marriage counseling session. I had the feeling that alcohol was the main cause of my marital problems. Dr. Modell confirmed that feeling when he said, "You two don't have a marital problem, you two have an alcohol problem."

While it is true that every drunk's story is different, some things are very common among alcoholics. We each tend to hit a variety of bottoms during our drinking career and we hit different levels and types of bottoms. For one person – peeing themselves, getting arrested for drunk driving or doing something embarrassing in public is a bottom – for another something like that is no big deal. Some drunks feel helpless, that there is nothing they can do and accept how their life is, some are fine living their life drunk. The fact is, some of us will never hit our bottom, never take control of our drinking, never do anything and simply die as a drunk. Hopefully you won't have to hit a catastrophic bottom. You might wake up one day and realize that you're done. Done with drinking, done with fucking up your life and done with fucking up other people's lives.

So my question to you is this: "What has to happen or what stupid thing must you do for you to hit your bottom?" Will it be an obvious event or will it be a series of smaller events that ultimately turn into a catastrophic crash? Some are easy to spot, such as getting arrested, killing someone by accident, getting fired, losing your house, having your partner leave you. Some bottoms are not so easy to spot. These include things like friends and family slowly drifting away from you, poor performance at your job, not taking care of your responsibilities or paying bills, always being broke and not remembering where you spent all your money, getting deeper and deeper into debt, letting your house and life become messy, casually compromising your morals or values, allowing your health to deteriorate, slowly gaining weight or not keeping yourself clean and presentable. It's the *quiet creeping bottoms* that we never see happening that are more problematic.

As drunks we all too often tell ourselves, "I'm not all that bad" and "I'll quit if something terrible ever happens." Guess what? If you wait for something terrible to happen, **it will**, and then it may be too late to ever recover from it. You don't have to wait for a traumatic, life-altering event to take place for you to hit bottom. I suggest that you spend some sober time to think honestly about whether your drinking is adversely affecting your life and relationships, then *ask yourself* the following questions:

- Do I think alcohol is a problem for me?
- Do I ignore my responsibilities?
- Do I always end up arguing with friends, partner or spouse when I drink?
- Do I drive drunk?
- Do people openly say "you drink too much"?
- Do I spend too much money on boozing?
- Do I have financial problems because I spend more money than I have – at the liquor store or bars?
- Do I completely forget what I did last night or forget entire weekends?
- Do I ever show up late for work because I was drinking the night before?
- Do I have a drink before work?
- Do I sneak a drink at lunch or during work?
- Do I go to work with a hangover?
- Do I have feelings of regret about things I did or said while I was drunk?
- Do I feel embarrassed about things I did while I was drunk?

- Do I feel like I am generally unlucky?
- Do I drink when I feel unlucky?
- Do I put myself in dangerous situations when I drink?
- Do I drink to relieve stress and problems?
- Do I have any personal goals other than getting drunk?
- Once I start drinking can I control how much I drink?
- Can I say, "No thank you" when offered a shot or a drink?
- Is my health suffering because of my drinking?
- Am I too skinny or too fat because of my drinking?
- Is there a lot of unnecessary drama and chaos in my life?
- Am I truly happy with how my life is and where it is going?
- Have I lost the respect of my friends, partner or children?
- Have I lost respect for myself?

These are only a few sample questions that you need to ask yourself. Being honest with yourself will be difficult, embarrassing and painful. As you review your answers you may become depressed, saddened by what you have done and what you have let your life become. The feeling of hopelessness may trigger your desire to drink right now – and if it does, that's a sure sign that you have a problem. **If you think you have an alcohol problem, then you probably already do have an alcohol problem**.

This is a very important mental exercise if you are going to stop drinking and start living sober. If you are serious about living sober, all I ask is that you truthfully answer these questions and don't hide from your answers or make excuses. Acknowledging to yourself that you do have an alcohol problem is only one part of the sobriety process but it can be the beginning of your turning point. Self-awareness is a sign of strength, but just being aware isn't going to change anything until you do something about it.

Your answers to these questions will give you some goals that you will want to achieve when you start your sober living. Examples of these goals might be: Never drive drunk again, get to work on time, find a better job, pay my bills, save money for something I want, further my education, exercise more. Having goals, reaching them and developing a reward system for yourself will build your resolve to stay sober and make it worth the effort. These concepts will be covered in the next few chapters.

At the very least consider living sober – what's the worst that can happen? Imagine how your life will improve, how healthy you will feel, how proud you will feel, how much better your friendships and relationships will be. Or do you want to keep drinking and living the way you are? I won't offer you false hope that by quitting drinking *everything* will get better and all that you have lost will be returned to you. But I can guarantee that *some* things will get better.

Don't wait to hit your final bottom before you do something about your drinking. You need to review what "bottoms" you have hit in the past. Have you had a lot of them? Too many to count? So many that it seems useless to even try to live sober? You may have gone down so far that some things can never be recovered, but you CAN salvage **yourself**.

#8) I am a freak of nature

This can be done by sheer willpower alone.

I am sorry to say this, but sometimes this sobering up shit sucks and life doesn't necessarily get any easier. But I'm sober and no one can take that away from me. I did it myself – which is why addiction and behavior counselors say **"You are a freak of nature."** I didn't do this for myself, I did it for all the people that I care about and for all the people that did not care about me (however I am ultimately reaping the benefits). I am very proud of what I have done and I don't think I am being conceited by constantly reminding myself how strong I am. I am not pounding my chest with bragging ego – but if I don't remind myself, I may let myself slip. My friends remind me how strong I am, how much power I possess and how much they admire my self-discipline. I think that's amazing and I am honored that people actually look up to me.

My thoughts on alcoholism and drug addiction, including my methods for recovery are unorthodox and will probably surprise you. I don't embrace the traditional recovery systems and many addiction specialists will disagree with me and my methods. Tough shit, this is my book. This process worked for me and continues to keep me sober. I believe that if you honestly want to sober up, it will work for you as well. I firmly believe that controlling your addictions can be done by using sheer willpower alone. I also believe that we all have the strength and willpower within ourselves.

71

Alcoholism isn't a disease - it's a choice. I choose if I want to drink or not. Can I control how much alcohol I will consume once I start drinking? No! It's alcohol – it gets me drunk. It makes my thought patterns get all fucked up, it assists me in making bad decisions, it makes dumb guys seem interesting, makes fat broads look attractive… that's its job, that's what alcohol is supposed to do. That's why I say that alcoholism isn't some horrible disease that can't be controlled. Nor do I buy into the lame excuse that alcoholics should be coddled, understood and have their actions overlooked. An alcoholic can be forgiven, but only after they have taken action to control their self-destructive behaviors. Alcoholism is your own choice, along with the recovery and controlling of your alcoholism.

If you are willing to agree with me that alcoholism is a choice, that means that you have also chosen a lifestyle that will lead you into bad behaviors and continued alcohol over usage. Alcohol will help you make poor personal and financial decisions. If you drink a lot of alcohol or if you drink daily, it will ultimately control your thoughts, emotions and relationships. From my own experience, the overuse of alcohol is something you choose to do, just as when you are choosing your clothes, your shoes or the car you want to buy. Choosing too much alcohol will have a negative effect on *all* of your other choices.

If you want to go with the argument that alcoholism is a disease, let's make a comparison. Let's assume that you were just told that you have a disease such as colon cancer, diabetes, sickle cell anemia or Parkinson's and you need treatment. You now have a choice. You can choose to go for treatment and cooperate with your doctor to control your disease – or not – that's your choice. If you choose not to go for treatment or try to control your disease, why should I feel compassion for you? You're being a fool. The same holds true for alcoholism. If it is clinically determined that you are an alcoholic or you can see that alcohol is ruining your life, then you have the choice to continue to drink or not to drink. I can talk boldly about this. I am an alcoholic and I made the choice whether I would continue to drink or not – I choose not to drink anymore.

Alcohol does not plan on taking control of your life. It has no feelings, no conscience, no soul. It also has no age, racial or gender boundaries. It can overtake any man or woman, no matter what race, religion, sexual preference or political party you are from. We are all truly equal when it comes to alcoholism.

Just because you're an alcoholic doesn't mean you are a bad individual loaded with personal flaws, faults and defects. Every drunk is not a jerk. We may do stupid things while we're drunk, but everything we do is not malevolent or done with underhanded intent. Some drunks are nice people that just do foolish things. On the other hand, what if you are a jerk? Does that mean you can't sober up unless you change who you are? Of course not. You can be a sober asshole all you want. You might be a grumpy boss or heartless business owner. Okay, stay that way, but you do have the power to be sober – and imagine how much better you could be at being mean and heartless if you were sober. Think of all the people you could belittle and humiliate, you could consider a career in politics. But in all sincerity, I am here to tell you that you don't have to change your character or eliminate all of your personal defects to become sober but you will have to change your personal destructive behaviors. If I can live sober and still maintain my character, you can too.

There are many internal and external elements that play a role in someone becoming an alcoholic. Our family, career choices, educational level, social status or financial status, geographical location, the people we hang out with and our own willingness to drink. Most people that drink start when they are in high school or college and then eventually grow out of it. Those of us that continue to drink in excess do so because we want to. Don't tell me, "I want to stop, I just can't." That's bullshit! You CAN stop. The truth is that you allow yourself to give in to temptation and

73

you talk yourself into justifying your drinking, then falling back on some lame-o excuse like, "it's a disease... have compassion on me." Fuck you! Do something about it if you want change. You will have to change the way you think and feel about alcohol, you will have to change the circumstances that influence you. You will have to consciously take control, make decisions and change your own life.

You might be willing to give up on yourself. Then do it. Go ahead, give up on yourself, and end it all now. If you do choose to commit suicide, please do so in a manner that causes the least amount of hardship to your family and society. Kill yourself in a fashion that doesn't cost your local government or community a lot of money. Fishing your rotting corpse out of a river without any identification costs the government money. Blowing your brains out in a motel room costs the motel owner money. He's got to have the room cleaned, needs a new mattress and you probably didn't pay for the room yet either. Please kill yourself in a clean, cost efficient way. Make certain that you have identification on you. Don't do a half-assed job at suicide. It's very expensive to have you end up in a hospital getting your stomach pumped or reconstructing your face because you're a bad aim with a handgun. Then there're the added costs of sending you through rehab and physical therapy. All for what? To have you attempt suicide again after you're able to be released? No thanks. If you're going to kill yourself, please do a professional job of it the first time. Good riddance!

You're still here? You decided against suicide? Fine, then let me ask you a question. How many times have you awoken in the morning feeling like shit? Both physically and emotionally because of stupid things you've done while you were drunk, and then told yourself, "I'm never drinking again." Then, in a few hours, days or weeks, you're right back at it, doing the same stupid shit again. If you've gotten this far in this book, it's probably because deep down inside you know that you have to quit or want to quit your destructive habits. I might have a sarcastic and sometimes cynical

74

attitude, (let's not forget my acerbic wit and natural modesty), but I would never deny another alcoholic my support and help. Even if I don't like you, I would never let that prevent me from helping you sober up – but that's only if YOU are sincere about wanting to live sober.

I am often asked the question: "What was the first thing you did when you quit drinking?" My answer: "I didn't drink anymore." Sounds simple, but that's the honest answer. However when I quit drinking I had no idea what I should do next, I had no idea what kind of psychological, physical and emotional torture I was about to go through.

I honestly thought that I could never live without alcohol. It physically hurt me to think about life without liquor. It was unimaginably emotional and mentally painful. My thoughts would start to race, wondering how I would ever cope with normal life. I wondered how I would deal with social activities, my friends, holidays. It was the physical *habit* of drinking that I was worried about. Then I would think about not ever getting buzzed again, which seemed even more impossible. What would life be like? I believed that there would be absolutely no way that I could, or would want to go through life without my friend alcohol. The thought of never drinking again scared the shit out of me but I knew I needed to stop – or as I foolishly thought – at least slow down a little. But I was so addicted to alcohol at the time that I had no idea how much I should limit myself to, or for how long I would have to cut down on my drinking. I had no idea where to start.

During the last few months of my drinking career life got pretty crazy. I had marital problems, I was deep in the midst of an Internet affair with Lorna, I wasn't paying attention to my job and I was drinking the heaviest I ever had in my life. I wouldn't start my day with the plan of getting completely drunk, but before I knew it, I was getting good and hammered again. I was pretty much fuckin' everything up. I had no control.

I would curtail my drinking for brief periods. I would cut back for a week or two; I even went an entire week without drinking any alcohol. I didn't experience tremors, shakes or see spiders during these short term *cut-down sessions*. I felt pretty normal. I discovered that you can quit drinking for short periods of time without suffering any physical or mental effects. I believe this is because your brain and body knows that you'll be drinking again soon. In any case, I would temper my drinking and drunkenness for a while, but then I would always end up getting way too drunk once again. I was like any typical drunk – quit or cut down for short periods of time, then make up for all the alcohol I missed out on by drinking even more the next time. Here's where you can't bullshit me and you shouldn't bullshit yourself. If you're an alcoholic you'll do the same thing I did – make up for what we missed out on. We eventually find our own level of how much we consume and then our addictive brain takes over and makes sure that we always drink up to, or a little beyond that level. What a crazy cycle we drunks go through.

There were only a few occasions (that I can remember) when people told me I was drinking too much – my doctor, my wife, my dad. It is interesting to reflect back on this now that I am sober. I don't recall these people suggesting that I quit drinking because I was an asshole or because they thought I was ruining my marriage, my career or my life. I was told I should quit for my own safety and health. Maybe they were just being nice and didn't want to tell me I was an asshole? For whatever reason, I still knew deep down inside that I had to stop drinking. I tried to deny it and lie to myself – but I knew the dark secret. I knew that I could achieve much more in my life if I could only curtail the amount I was drinking. I was so good at hiding how adversely alcohol was affecting my life. I hid it so well that even I believed it.

I am living proof that being an alcoholic will slowly fuck up your life. Once it starts, the ball begins rolling and it gets going faster and faster. Once alcoholism hits a certain speed, there's no stopping it and suddenly everything gets smashed and crushed that is in its way. Sometimes you're lucky enough to have someone point out your impending demise. Sometimes the people that are involved in your life will force you to see what is coming your way. Too often the alcoholic isn't willing to listen to anyone and it runs right over you and crushes your life's dreams.

I finally came to the realization that I had to stop drinking. I have been able to quit many bad habits in my life and have taken on many good habits. I figured this would be easy, everything would get better and my life would become magically wonderful. Holy shit was I wrong!

Upon quitting drinking I also went after a new career in a very demanding and stressful industry. I started making a good income, I was paying off debt, I was trying to change myself so I would become a better husband and a better person. I piled a lot of stress upon myself and undertook a lot of tough projects. I tried to repair my marriage, but I ended up being dumped by my wife anyway. I felt weak and unwanted and I had lost my self confidence. I had to keep myself from drinking and falling down into a pit of depression. And all I really had at that time was myself.

I still have difficulty believing and understanding how *bad* of a person I was as a drunk. I probably wasn't as bad a person as others have made me out to be. I was not a vicious, rotten, violent drunk. I may not have gotten into bar fights, fights with family or friends, I didn't get arrested, I didn't lose my job, lose my house, lose all my money, lose my family. None of these things happened to me directly because of my drinking, but *indirectly* I eventually lost all of these things. With hard work, dedication, good friends and a bit of luck, I have been able to get most of these things back. I even have more of these things now. I have talked with a lot of people who have lost all of these things and did do a lot of bad shit while they were drunk. Every drunk has a different story and has done different things to harm themselves and others. But we're all still the same at the core… we're all drunks.

I had to forgive myself and learn to face the current consequences of my behaviors. I hear people say: "Whatever happens in life will be the best for you." Well my response to that is: "Fuck You! How the fuck do you know what would be the best for me? Bad shit happens to good people and good shit happens to bad people. There is no balance or ledger system in life."

You also will have to forgive yourself and promise yourself that you WILL be a better person in the future. You will have to try and get over whatever bad stuff happened and make good with people you have harmed. It may not work, some people may not care that you want to make good, it honestly may be too late. You are the only person that can help you. It sounds easier said than done and some of what you will go through isn't fair. It's easy to talk when it's not happening to the person giving feedback or advice. But hey, I lived this bullshit, I've been through the pain, I've battled through the mental torture I imposed upon myself, I have experienced the psychological anguish, racing thoughts, contemplation of suicide, feeling that life didn't matter. I have cried myself to sleep – when I actually could sleep – I have woke up crying, I hated myself for every bad thing I did as a drunk,,,, I have been to HELL (and it's not a very nice place - it's hot and there's no windows).

I am honest with you by saying that this is not going to be easy. There is absolutely no doubt that this will be difficult. Believe me when I tell you that it will be hard, real fucking hard. It will probably be the hardest thing you will ever do in your life and you will have to do it on your own.

Here is a preview: You're going to feel anger, resentment, emotional pain, physical pain, weakness, self-doubt, boredom, hatred… and that's just in the first hour of sobriety. I'm not trying to talk you out of this or make you think that it's too much work or not worth the effort. It is worth the effort for many reasons. The positive reasons are limitless: the better standard of life that you and your family will enjoy, the new level of self-confidence that you will enjoy, the pride that will emanate from you when you are able to tell people that you sobered up all on your own. People that knew you as a drunk or an addict will see you as an entirely different person. They will have a newfound respect for you on higher levels. You are not a better person than anyone else is, but inside you can feel as if you are.

If you continue to approach your life in the same way, doing the same things, going to the same places, then you can expect the same results. If you continue going to bars, hanging out with your drinking buddies, doing the same social routines, chances are good you will continue to drink. You can still do all the same things you always did, hang out with some of your old friends and NOT drink; it just takes your own willpower to say "NO" to drinking. (I'll be giving you some techniques on how to do this in coming chapters.) I'll admit that it's easier to stay sober when you're not in a bar or have temptation paraded in front of you, so why put yourself through the torture of temptation? My worst hell isn't the immediate temptation itself; it's the creeping temptation afterwards. Temptation hits me an hour later, once I've gone home, or the next day when I start thinking that I could drink "just a couple." You know what? I probably could drink just a couple, but it wouldn't be fun for me. So I'm better off not drinking at all. That's the harsh reality and attitude you need to embrace and welcome into your life. It's okay to say it and even remind yourself "I probably could drink just a couple, but it wouldn't be any fun for me. So I'm better off not drinking at all."

There are many reasons why I stay sober and one of them is spite. The pure joy of proving people wrong has kept me sober longer than anything else. I revel in the knowledge that some people were dead-wrong about me. Not only do they see that I am able to maintain my sobriety, but they see that I live a healthier, fun and successful life. I stay sober so I can metaphorically stick my success up their asses. Are my motives wrong or shallow? I don't believe so. Enough people tried to undermine my efforts, stab me in the back and piss in my well. Anger and spite are real human emotions and can be used to propel you along to achieve your goal of sobriety. But don't allow these emotions to overtake you and run your life. It's counterproductive to your sobriety if you go out of your way to seek vengeance on others (some of your actions might be illegal too). Don't let anger or spite become a misdirected destructive force against innocent bystanders. I support a good balance of both positive and negative emotions.

Please don't interpret me as bitter. I cherish my loving family and friends, I am rewarded with people that believe in me and care about me. But in my own perverse way, it comforts me to know that anyone that didn't ever think I was worth a fuck, can now look at me and see a happier, stronger, sober person. The best revenge is letting others see me live well. Many people said, "Oh, Mark will never stay sober." Those would include my wife's horse riding friends, some of my in-laws, and generally people that didn't like me in the first place. How many people will be saying that about you? Well, fuck 'em... fuck 'em all. **Prove to those people that they are wrong about you.** Show them that you are far stronger than they think you are, and prove to yourself that *you* care about you.

The goal of sobriety is not to torture yourself, to suffer and feel pain – the goal is to make a better life for yourself and the people you love. You owe it to yourself, your family, friends, employer, coworkers and your customers. It's easy to compile statistics through internet searches (but a boring pain in the ass) about recovered drunks. Most have higher success rates with their marriages and make more money than average. This is due to their higher levels of dedication, strengthened work ethics, clearer financial goals and better health. I hope your relationships or marriage gets better after you start to live sober. I hope you enjoy your children more and they enjoy you more. I hope you make a lot more money so you can treat your family and friends to the comforts and conveniences that money and sobriety can bring. I hope you have far better success at all these things than I ever will.

If you have a spouse, partner or lover and you are going to commit to living sober, then you are going to embark on a new way of life that can be filled with joy, happiness, fulfillment and great expectations. Every day can be a fabulous experience if you have someone to help you with your goal of sobriety. There will also be times of stress, struggle, anger, boredom and frustration, but that's what life is.

It takes willpower to see that you have a problem. It takes willpower to accept that you must do something about it. It takes willpower to take control of your life and take control over destructive habits. It takes even more willpower to stay vigilant and not fall back into easy patterns and old destructive habits. My willpower is fed by my various emotions; Anger, spite, self-esteem, personal pride, fear, guilt, joy, self-love and love for others. I will elaborate more on how to muster up your own willpower in coming chapters.

I sobered up without going to rehab, following any 12-step recovery program, going to meetings or the help and support of a loving partner. I actually had the person that I trusted, loved and needed the most, undermine me and torment me along the way, which made this even harder. I did this solely on my own. I am not a special person; I have no special talent, strength or skill. But if I can do this on my own, I know that you can do it too. I may be a freak of nature, but so are you.

#9) Let's get started, shall we?

A brief overview of what is to come.

But first, a little history on alcohol in the U.S.A. In 1826 (almost 100 years *before* Prohibition) the American Temperance Society was founded to convince people to abstain from drinking. The anti-Saloon League was formed in 1893 and eventually became a very powerful political force. In 1917, the House of Representatives wanted to make Prohibition the 18th Amendment to the Constitution. The amendment stipulated a time limit of seven years for the states to pass this amendment. In just 13 months (and you thought our government rams shit through too quickly now) enough states said yes to this amendment and on October 18, 1919 Congress passed the Volstead Act – officially titled the National Prohibition Act. February 1, 1920 "Prohibition" went into effect as a law. This made it illegal to manufacture, sell and transport alcoholic liquors. Personal consumption of alcohol was not clearly stated to be "illegal," but the law was constructed so that anyone in possession of alcohol was in violation because possession was construed as "intent to deliver" (hey pot-heads, sound familiar?).

People still continued to drink. In fact, by 1925, it was estimated that New York City had anywhere from 30,000 to 100,000 speakeasy clubs. Neither federal nor local authorities committed the resources necessary to enforce the Volstead act. The state of

Maryland refused to pass any enforcement issue. All prohibition did was create an opportunity for bootleggers and crime to become profitable and well... organized.

On February 20, 1933 the 21st Amendment passed, which repeals the 18th Amendment. December 5, 1933 people could legally buy alcohol once again.

Prohibition didn't work then and it won't work now. Just because you and I might not be able to control our drinking, why should we require other people to live by our rules? People are going to drink whether we want them to or not. Some people will become alcoholics, ruin their own lives, families, marriages, careers, etc., whether alcohol is legal or not.

I want to state again that this book is the story of what *I did* to control and ultimately stop my drinking. These are the things that worked for me. These are also the things that didn't work for me. My technique may work better for you than it did for me – I hope it does. My style may not work for you at all. Just the fact that you're reading this and you're willing to try something is a promising sign. I am not an accredited therapist, I have not been formally educated or trained with regard to substance and alcohol abuse. I only know what I was able to do for myself – quit drinking and learn to live sober – by accepting harsh realities and reliance on my own willpower.

I do not have a series of steps, a system or guaranteed program that you can follow. I will not be telling you, "Okay, if you do this first, this second and this third you will cure your addiction." I will tell you that if you are seriously planning on living sober, then there is ONLY one step that you must do and that step is to NOT drink alcohol. I am about to share with you the various stages I went through. Every drunk and every situation is different, which is why I don't claim to have a system or program that is guaranteed to work. All I can do is share with you some examples of what to expect and give you some ideas that you might want to try.

I suggest that as you are reading, you highlight some of the ideas that you think will work for you. Have a notepad available so you can write out your own goals and plan for achieving these goals. It is necessary to have a plan to accomplish your goals – and one of those goals is to live sober. Writing a plan will get you involved in your recovery and it will help you take this process seriously. Your own written goals will give you something to refer back to when you question whether this is worth the effort. Your written plans will help refocus your thoughts when you are unsure about how to handle the struggles and temptations that you will undoubtedly encounter – *because living sober is not a onetime event, it is a lifelong project* (please highlight that). Your own written goals will be a nice thing to go back and read after you have been sober for a month, three months, six months… years later. So let's get started shall we?

Drinking is a choice. I have stated this earlier – I choose to live sober or to drink. You may tell me that your mind wants to quit but your body won't let you or that you have no willpower or you can't control your urge to drink. Drinking and drugs may cause physical dependencies, but the choice is still a MENTAL decision. Drinking becomes a routine that overtakes your every thinking decision – I know this from my own experience. **But a single act of willpower can alter your thinking and change the choices and decisions you make for the rest of your life.** As you digest this concept, I hope that you begin to understand that we make up all kinds of excuses for drinking – "I'm under stress, I have low self-esteem, I was abused, I'm an alcoholic, etc." Drinking is completely **your own choice**. You can choose to not go to a bar. You can choose to not stop at the liquor store or gas station. You can choose to say, "No thank you" when someone offers you a drink.

I will agree that outside influences can persuade you to drink – friends, family, spouse, and advertising. I understand that you have the urge to drink. But these urges are just thoughts; it is your own mind talking you into drinking. You have the choice as to whether you will take action on these thoughts and urges or not. You consciously choose to physically to go buy beer, wine or liquor, to stop at a bar, whatever. Unless someone ties you down and forcibly pours alcohol into your mouth, **you have the choice to drink or not drink**, regardless of how addicted you are. You are ultimately the only one making this choice. Alcohol only assists in making your other choices – dumb choices at that – once it is in your bloodstream. And it can only get into your bloodstream once you have made the conscious choice to introduce it into your body.

You therefore have **the power of choice** in starting and maintaining your sobriety. You have the choice in how you undertake this process. You have the choice of who you will hang out with and surround yourself with. Counseling can help, therapy can help, support groups can help, a 12-Step program can help. Ultimately you make the choice whether you are going to drink or not – it is completely up to you. If you can agree with me that this is a choice, honestly embrace the fact that you are solely responsible for your own decisions, then you can learn techniques and strategies to help you control your thoughts and actions to make the right choice.

I will be the first to admit that simply agreeing that drinking is a choice won't make this an easy process. What it will do is allow you to undertake an honest approach. My hope for you is that it will remind you that you do in fact have more control over alcohol than you think (or want to admit). Over the next few weeks and months when temptation strikes (and it will) you can remind yourself that sobriety is YOUR choice and that you are the only person that can choose whether you will be a slave to alcohol.

Change is a constant variable, so accept change as your friend. If you are a drunk or a drug addict, you'll be a drunk or a drug addict wherever you go. Moving to a different city, state, country or planet won't change you. You have to change some of your current habits along with changing your attitude and feelings about alcohol/drugs. If you are surrounded by drunks and drug addicts, chances are good that you will continue to be one yourself, so it might be necessary for you to change your social and geographical environment. Removing yourself from those unhealthy environments will help put the obvious temptations out of sight, but you still have to take control of your habits and choices. It's not easy. (For me, it was far easier being a drunk – I didn't give a shit about anyone or anything else. I'm just being honest.)

The simple truth is that whether you continue drinking and doing drugs or not, change *will* happen to you and around you. If you're drunk at the time that change is occurring, you either won't see it happening or change will be out of your control. As a drunk, the changes that will probably happen are things like: losing your job, house, wife, husband, partner, friends, family, money, respect of others, and driver's license... the list could go on for pages.

If you do decide to change your drinking habits to live clean and sober, then expect the unexpected. People are going to treat you differently, especially your "drinking buddies", and I can't guarantee that people will treat you any better. Change will occur within you as well. You will think differently, act differently and *you* will treat people differently. Many of these changes will not be what you want or what you are expecting. Some changes will be good and some will be painful, however, as a sober person, YOU will be the one in control of how you react to change.

These are some of the changes you can expect. (More about the emotional and psychological changes you will go through, along with tips on how to deal with them will be covered later). At first, all you will think and talk about is your recovery – you will be obsessed with it. You will be tempted to preach your *new religion* of sobriety to everyone you know and meet. You will also notice how other people act when they are drunk. You might begin to find drunk people disgusting or pathetic. Conversely, you may even be jealous or get angry at people who still drink. You might have feelings that you are better than drunks. Well, you're not – you are

87

not superior to anyone else – you're just a normal person that has self control who doesn't drink.

During the early days of sobriety (first 7 to 30) you will be easily irritated and agitated. You will probably be hypersensitive. You will overreact to comments people make. Your friends, family, coworkers will be easy targets for you to unleash your anger upon. Simple things will get you mad and pleasurable activities may not seem very exciting. You will have feelings of depression, sadness and might become lethargic. You might find work and life in general to be boring. (Alcohol covered up the boredom. Remember how you could sit around drinking for hours and do absolutely nothing, but you still weren't bored? Alcohol numbs your brain and makes dumb people and dumb shit seem interesting.) You will have difficulty thinking clearly when you first sober up. You might have multiple thoughts racing through your mind. You might find that as you're sobering up you don't like some of your old friends anymore, and they might not like you. That's okay, it's all part of the change.

If you're married or living with someone, things might get really rough for a while. Your spouse/partner may not understand the agony you are going through. Just because you decided to sober up doesn't wipe out all the rotten shit you may have done to them in the past. Just because you are sorry doesn't mean that you are forgiven. In fact you may never be forgiven. The dynamics of your relationship will change. Hopefully it will change for the better. Your partner may not be as excited about your new sobriety as you are. They may not be as supportive of you as you thought they would be. They might be thankful for this change and embrace you with a new sense of love and respect, but don't expect or demand this from them. Remember that YOU are changing and they may have never known you as a sober person. It took time for you to become a drunk, it will take time for your mind and your life to become accustomed to the change of being sober.

Your new sober life will not be limited to this list of changes. You may experience some of these changes, all of these changes or none of them, but change will happen in your life no matter what you do. If you continue to drink and/or do drugs, life will change around you and those changes will most likely be for the worse. If you do stop drinking and/or doing drugs, changes will happen as well, however you will be in a better position to make those changes work in your favor. Take control of your life and take control of the inevitable changes that are headed your way.

Be selfless and live sober for someone else: Many people will say that you have to sober up for "you". They will say that you can't do it for someone else. I disagree. I think you can live sober for someone else. I would rather be drinking. I like to drink, I like the taste of beer and alcohol. I am honest with myself, this helps me respect what alcohol is and what it does to a person. I am living sober for other people, not for me.

Let me give you an example. I had a wonderful wife and we lived a charmed life and I stopped drinking for her, hoping it would save my marriage. Well my marriage still came to a sad, foolish, unnecessary ending – at least I think so, my ex might say otherwise. But I have no regrets for sobering up for her and trying to salvage my marriage. I have no regrets for sobering up for someone else and I have no resentment for it either. I am ultimately living with the rewards of my sobriety, even though I did it for someone else.

I see the joy on peoples' faces when I talk with them and have deep, fun conversations. I remember how proud my dad felt that I was strong enough to sober up. I like being invited to parties and events because I'm a fun person and not because I have good drugs or I'm a good drinker. I like knowing that other people are jealous that I have the strength to control my drinking. I enjoy knowing that because I am sober and still alive, this pisses some people off. I like the fact that I scare some people with my honesty and ability to control my urges to drink again. I like knowing that I can be an inspiration to others and that they just might have better lives and better relationships because of me. I stay sober for everyone else but me.

I do not feel let down by sobriety. I would be lying and misleading you if I told you that sobriety is going to be a totally wonderful experience, filled with joy, love, happiness and heightened levels of consciousness – it's not. It's just normal life filled with good times and bad times. When we get drunk, we feel "high." There is no equal and opposite sensation for sobriety. I don't feel a sobriety buzz. I will say that I am more aware of things happening around me. I make better decisions (or I should say fewer bad decisions), I am better at my work and can enjoy my career more. I am less irritable and I am not as easily rattled by trivial difficulties that are inevitable in life.

So are you ready to change your life and live sober? Once you start your new way of sober living, it may throw a lot of things in your life out of balance. Any change you make will have a direct impact on many people. Even positive changes may create problems. Some people won't be as excited for you to sober up, some may not think you should change or want you to change. Some of your friends may resent you because you are able to do something that they can't, or they might resent you because they just lost their drinking buddy. Your desire to change may upset a lot of people. Are you ready for this? This is a huge, life altering decision. Your spouse or partner may say they want you to quit drinking/drugs, but when the rough spots happen, they may not be able to help. They may not know what to say; they may not understand what is so hard or why you are so irritable. They may even say that they want "the old you back."

Luck isn't personal. *Good luck* and *bad luck* is NOT personal. As the saying goes – Shit happens. The universe doesn't conspire to help or hinder you. But so often *bad luck* is a result of our own actions, a result of where we are and what we are doing within our lives. When I drank I always felt as if *bad luck* had singled me out.

What I perceived as bad luck only made me more depressed, then I drank more, bringing on even more bad luck. Or what was even more dangerous – when I was drunk – I would feel a delusional sense that I would be lucky, or that *good luck* would come my way, then I did even more risky things, resulting in even more bad luck.

You might be asking, "Okay Mark, what does luck have to do with alcoholism?" Here's my answer: What we alcoholics perceive as *bad luck* is actually the unfortunate results of our own drunken actions. I further believe that you can improve your life and change your luck by changing your drinking habits. When you drink or do drugs in excess, unfortunate things happen and *bad luck* will come your way. (By the way, the dictionary considers both "luck" and "fortunate" as interchangeable words, but I feel that they are distinctively different words regarding the good and bad events that happen in our lives.)

For example, you are not unlucky because you got arrested for drunk driving. What occurred is *unfortunate* but you certainly are not *unlucky*. You were in control of the situation and you happened to be drunk. You were – on the other hand – *lucky* for not being arrested all the other hundreds of times you were driving drunk. The same goes if you get caught bangin' your neighbor's wife – that's not *bad luck*, that's *misfortune* – because you were in control of the situation, you could have passed on the opportunity. So let me repeat this – **what we drunks perceive as *bad luck* is actually *unfortunate* results of our own actions**.

I believe that many aspects of luck are well within our own control. If you hang out in bars, hang out with drunks and surround yourself with drug addicts, *bad luck* is probably going to come your way. I am not inferring that if you quit drinking your life will suddenly be filled with *good luck* and you'll win the lottery. I can't guarantee anything like that, but I can guarantee you this – if you don't drink, you can't get arrested for drunk driving.

I believe that by living sober – staying away from high-risk and chaotic environments, you will create the opportunity for *good luck* events to take place more often in your life, and have fewer occurrences of *bad luck* happen to you. Keep in mind that even after you quit drinking, occurrences of bad luck will still happen to you, but you will be in a better position to handle them. Remember that *good luck* as well as *bad luck* is NOT personal – luck is just something that happens to all of us. So why not stack the laws of probability in your favor? Control and eliminate the opportunities for *bad luck* to happen to you and enable the chances of *good luck* to come your way.

On that note, I will say that I don't believe in karma, kismet, Ju-Ju or whatever you want to call it. Bad luck is not balanced out with equal eventuations of good luck. Luck – good and bad – is just a part of life. I do firmly believe that at some point alcoholism will catch up with you and *consequences* will have to be paid. My best buddy Mike said it so eloquently when he stated, "In life, everybody's bill eventually comes due." Mike is so right. *I am paying the price today for what I did yesterday*. It's just something to think about.

No one can actually force you to sober up. Sure, you may get forced into rehab by your employer, your family or by the courts because you were arrested again, but you will not sober up until YOU decide that you are willing to. And you can't expect others to keep you sober or hold them responsible for keeping you sober. This is completely up to you. You may be staying sober for someone else, but they can't do it for you, only you can do it. Some days will be easy, some days not so easy. Living sober can be much less of a challenge and far more rewarding if you are doing it with someone like a spouse, lover, friend or partner and you have specific goals in mind.

Stop thinking and just do it! I can't stress enough that if you **think** you have an alcohol or drug problem, then you probably **do** have a problem. Don't end up like me. I am glad that I am sober, but I did it too late. I lost the greatest thing that ever happened to me in my life, I lost my wife. I may be sad and lonely at times, but I am sober. I will not blame the alcohol for what happened. I made the choice to drink and to continue drinking in a super-human fashion. I live with that guilt every day. I am tormented with nightmares. How could I have fucked up such a wonderful thing? I understand what I did, I accept what I did, but I still can't do anything to get back what I lost.

All I can say is that I wish I would have sobered up sooner. It may have saved my marriage. I didn't see all the signs in front of me. I can only imagine how annoying I must have been. I'm sure I brought terrible anxiety upon my wife. Not just with my daily drunken drama, but having her always wonder how drunk I was going to get or how drunk I would be when I got home. I can clearly see that this was too much bullshit for anyone to put up with. Sadly, once I decided to sober up it was too late. My wife was done with all of my drunkenness. I am heartbroken, struggling with the guilt of hurting her. Don't do this to yourself or to the person you love. If you are thinking about learning to live sober, all I can say is, "stop thinking and just do it!"

Living sober is not a onetime event, it is an ongoing process, it is a continuous change in your way of life. You can't hurry or rush sobriety along. I could hardly wait to say "30 days sober." No matter how much I rushed it, it still took 30 days. And once I hit 30 days did I experience some great reward or fabulous sensation? NO – it was just another day. That's all that sobriety is… just another day of my life… but I was sober. If you're going to go without drinking and live sober, try it for at least 30 days. You will have to go "one day at a time," to eventually reach 30 days. But nothing counts unless you try it for at least 30 days, then another 30 days, etc. You might have to start by going sober a night here, a weekend there, but I ask that you eventually go sober for 30 days. Be selfless and live sober for someone else. Try it for 30 days. What's the worst that can happen?

#10) Okay wise guy, how do I do this?

This is going to hurt.

Up to this point I have talked about why we drink, how it might be adversely effecting our lives and listed some reasons why you might want to stop drinking. You may have spent time reflecting on some of the dumb shit you have done and whether you feel as if you have hit your own bottom. I have shared my opinions on alcoholism, personal responsibility and willpower. I have also brought to light some of the challenges and struggles you will undoubtedly face while going through recovery and some of the changes that you can expect.

People like simple and easy answers, but these two words *simple & easy* don't equate to one another when it comes to sobriety. Living sober can be a *simple* task but it will not be an *easy* task. It is *simple* in that all you need to do is not drink, yup, that's the simple part. Controlling your urges and temptations to drink or do drugs will not be *easy*.

So here is the *simple* plan that I developed for myself and followed to achieve sobriety. I will be detailing the actions I undertook. I made changes in my activities and attitude along the way – adapting myself and my plan – based upon what was working and what wasn't working for me. I will share my experiences of success and failure. I will speak of the difficulties and mistakes I made. I will tell you about what painful conditions I encountered and the psychological confusion I felt and still feel.

"I'm ready to start living sober, how do I do this?"

Pick a date that you will stop drinking. A lot of times you don't have a choice on picking your own date. You may get arrested, end up in a hospital due to your alcoholism, get sent off to rehab, be the recipient of an intervention or have some other catastrophic event occur in your life.

If you have the luxury of picking your own stop date, plan for this date to be about a month from now. If you can plan to do it sooner or you have decided that right now is the best time, all the better. The reason I suggest a date in the near future is so you can reflect on why you want to quit, prepare yourself mentally and emotionally. You'll want to detail out a personal plan and write out your goals. This will also give you time to be seen by a physician if you feel that is necessary. Your doctor may recommend some medications to aid with physical withdrawals, irritability or potential sleep and appetite difficulties. If you do go to see a doctor, be completely honest about your alcohol or drug consumption.

Set your **stop date** for a day at the end of a weekend or early in the week, like a Sunday or a Monday. This way when you stop drinking, the next few days won't be such a big temptation because you will have three to five days that will keep you busy with work, projects, school or job hunting if you're unemployed.

Personal experience: When I decided that I would quit, I mentally began planning on having a big "going dry" party – spending two solid days getting drunk on Scotch and beer. Think about what I just said. Isn't it sad that I was planning to completely waste two or three days of my life so I could get drunk, probably get sick, and then feel like shit for a day or two afterwards, to celebrate that I was quitting. Sounds stupid to me now but it sure

96

made sense to me before I quit drinking. I never did have my party. In hindsight I'm glad that I didn't. This might sound a bit crazy, but some people may want to host a "going dry" party and invite all of their drinking friends. I don't recommend this, but some of us need closure when saying goodbye to an old friend. If you're going to do this, have your party the weekend you quit drinking. Get so drunk that you make a total ass out of yourself. Get sick, throw up on yourself, poop your pants, and maybe even get arrested. That might be what it takes for you to finally come to grips with your problem.

Write your stop date down and circle it on a calendar that you look at frequently. You don't have to tell anyone what the circled date means. In fact I suggest that you keep your plan and your stop date private – don't tell anyone else just yet. The reason you don't want to tell anyone yet is because they will be excited for you and they might ask you, "Why wait? Why not quit right now?" This will only heap more pressure on you. Then as you explain your plan to them it will simply sound like you're making excuses. Drinking partners won't be supportive of your plan; they won't want you to quit drinking, so they will try talking you out of it. Or what happens when you end up talking with friends and family about your plan to quit drinking – while you're still actively drinking? There is nothing more ridiculous than listening to a drunk person tell you how they're going to quit drinking – *while they're having another drink*. Most people are going to have a hard time believing you and you sound pretty stupid doing it. I think you're better off telling as few people as possible.

Personal experience: Why you should keep your plan private. When I told my wife that I was quitting drinking she was unimpressed – she planned on continuing to drink. In fact, on my second day of sobriety we went out for dinner and she told me "quit being such a big baby and have a beer." I can't blame her, I was already starting to go through alcohol withdrawal and neither one of us knew what kind of hellish journey I had just begun.

97

Starting TODAY, begin a daily cutting back of your consumption. Have one less drink every day this week, then one less drink every day next week, etc. Switch to a brand or flavor that isn't appealing to you – this will help you control your urge to "have another one." During this time period don't sit and think about never drinking again, just pay attention to your daily consumption and cutting back on it. As your stop date approaches be sure to let your inventory of booze dwindle down. Only have enough beer or booze in the house that will get you through a single day. You will notice that you're already spending less money.

At some point you are going to have to bare your soul and expose your plan to another person, but be very careful who you do this with. I know that it's exciting to tell everyone about your plans for living sober. Remember that most people won't care and some may even try to talk you out of it or you may have made this promise many times in the past and no one will believe you anyway. You don't want to set yourself up for ridicule – you want to set yourself up to succeed! You will have plenty of time to announce that you are living sober – like after your first 30 days – in fact you will have the rest of your life to announce this. If you are married or have a partner or roommate that will be supportive, tell them a week ahead of your stop date so they are ready to help you when that final night arrives. Yes, there will be a final night when you say *goodbye* to your old friend alcohol.

When your stop date has arrived, it's now time to start your new life. Your spouse, partner, friend or lover needs to play a huge role in your healing – plan to spend the next few evenings together. I can't stress enough how important a role your spouse or partner is going to play in your sober life. If you don't have a partner, plan to spend the next few evenings with a friend or family. Go to their house for dinner, make them dinner, or go out to eat (and nobody drinks). On those first few nights you can watch movies, play table games, computer games, talk, read a book. Do some busy-work around the house – laundry, wash dishes, vacuum, make lunches for the week, rearrange cupboards or closets, whatever. It sounds boring (and it will be at times) but this is your own life that you are saving. The first 72 hours are the hardest, most important and most crucial hours. Let me repeat this because it is that important. *The first 72 hours are the hardest, most important and most crucial hours.*

Here is why this time frame is so crucial: During the first 72 hours your body will be clearing alcohol out of your system. Drink a lot of water or Cranberry juice to help flush it out (avoid soda and coffee – the caffeine will make you more fidgety and anxious). You will be peeing a lot, but so what – you peed a lot when you drank. Mental urges to drink will be at their highest. These urges are just thoughts – unconscious thoughts – that will invade your conscious thinking. These unconscious thoughts will be driving you to fulfill the physical habit of drinking – which in turn introduces the mind-altering substance back into your bloodstream. If you crack, you will psychologically feel week and helpless. You will mentally reconfirm to yourself that you have no control. Exerting conscious control over these unconscious thoughts will keep you from physically introducing alcohol back into your system. Psychologically you will then feel stronger. If you don't mentally feel strong, then consciously remind yourself of your strength – how you have been able to have power over these urges. 72 hours will allow your mind and body to begin clearing itself of the influences of alcohol.

Stay busy: Time will drag and each minute that ticks by will feel like an eternity if you are consciously thinking about it. When you start your sobriety, make sure that you have a busy schedule planned. If you can work extra hours, do so. If you can fill in for someone, do so. If you can get a second job, take it. I made sure that I was working 60 or more hours a week. I had no time for a personal life, I didn't do anything but work and sleep. You have to stay busy. Immersing yourself in your work, schooling or hobbies for the next few months will save your life. If you can't work extra hours, then join a health club or go volunteer for a church, school or neighborhood project. If you can help it, don't just stay at home. Being alone allows your mind to wander and the temptation to drink will haunt you. You want to make sure that you are around other people. They don't have to know why you're working so many hours or why you're volunteering.

Most other recovering drunks would agree that it's easier to stay sober if you're busy at work, doing something or you're somewhere that you can't drink. Being at work, keeping busy with projects and hobbies will keep your mind off of alcohol.

If you have children, a spouse, partner or other family obligations, you might not be able to work more hours. In that case, spend sober time with your kids, spouse, partner or your family. Do something to stay busy. Idle time is dangerous, your mind starts wandering. You start thinking about the wrong things. Examples of wrong thoughts include: reminiscing about drinking activities, replaying mistakes from your past – guilt, remembering bad things that have been done to you, being jealous of others who still drink and all of the fun you *think* they are having, thinking in terms of self-pity because you no longer drink, feelings of boredom. I have to constantly remind myself to keep busy and think the right kind of thoughts. Sober and alone is not fun for me; I am not used to living this way. My imagination takes off on its own and then there are too many radio stations playing in my head at one time.

If you are in a relationship, plan on spending time together doing things and going places that don't revolve around drinking. Spend more time being involved with daily chores. Clean the house together, do the laundry together, go grocery shopping together, go for walks together, go to the library and read books together, play Yahtzee or have sex. If you have children, spend more time being involved with their education, sports, school events and interests.

Personal experience: My spouse didn't help me through my early stages of sobriety. My wife berated and tormented me for

100

quitting drinking. She would get drunk and make fun of me, call me weak, pathetic, no fun, and did this all while I was going through my hardest hours, days, weeks and months. I needed her help desperately, but she turned on me. I am not trying to speak ill of her or spew my sour grapes, I am telling you this so you understand that **no matter what anyone does to you or says to you, no matter how painful – you can stay sober**. I hope that your spouse, lover or partner will be there to help you. If they stick with you through all of this, you better be good to them in return. They shouldn't hold their support over your head as a bargaining tool or as a way to make you feel guilty. But nonetheless, you will owe them your life! Tell them how much you love them and thank them every day for their help.

Consider reading self-improvement books as a way to keep busy. You can make becoming a better person part of your goal and part of your sobering up plan. Working on becoming a better person will consume a lot of your thinking time and help direct what kind of activities you participate in. From my own experience, when actively working at being a better person is the focus of my thoughts, it is easier to control my urges to drink. But being a better person is not a requisite to sobriety. Some may disagree with me and say that all you have become is a "dry drunk." You can still live sober – even if you like being a jerk. This subject will be touched on later.

Prepare your body for sleep: You may encounter difficulty sleeping when you first quit. Restless nights, shakes, sweating and insomnia. Staying busy during the day and getting physically exhausted will help. But you need to get some solid rest. Don't lay in front of the TV hoping to fall asleep. Go lie down in bed and prepare your body for sleep. Get comfortable and read. Read a magazine or a book. I recommend books on positive psychology (Malcolm Gladwell, Dale Carnegie, Dr. Wayne Dyer, Alan Cohen, Richard Carlson, to name a few). Or simply lay there with your eyes closed and review what you accomplished during the day. Do not review errors of your past. Mentally plan out what you will do tomorrow. With your eyelids closed, direct your eyes upward and to the right and project loving visions and thoughts towards the people you care about. This sounds boring but it will help you relax and tire you out, which will help you get a good night sleep.

Exercise: Not only will exercising take up more of your time and be a distraction from your desire to drink, it will help build self-confidence, positively affect your health and assist in sleeping better. Exercising will improve your mood by releasing endorphins. Endorphins are released by your pituitary glands. Lifting weights will strengthen and tone the body, but it will not release as many endorphins. Intense aerobic exercises are more likely to release these than just lifting weights. If you are going to lift weights, do that first, then follow-up with 10-20 minutes of running, swimming or spinning to help release endorphins.

Change your environments: Here's an obvious one – stay out of bars for a while. I also suggest that for the first 30-90 days you place yourself into a self-imposed lockdown. Stay away from social environments that have alcohol associated with them. This might include sporting events, concerts, parties or after work gatherings. Make yourself unavailable for random friends to drop by and hang out with you. Associate with only the closest people in your life. You need to get through your initial sobering up period with a few close friends. If you are single and you're going to stay at home then read or go over to a friend's house that knows you are not drinking. Once you have a few weeks of sobriety under your belt you might be ready to venture out into social settings that have alcohol. At that point you can tell people about your sobriety. Tell them that you are NOT going to drink. Ask them to please not tempt you, ask them to not treat you any differently. Most of all, ask them to hold you accountable for sticking to your word and for being accountable for yourself. Let them know that you don't expect them to keep you sober. Your sobriety is NOT anyone else's responsibility… it's yours!

Personal experience: I didn't stay away from my drinking buddies for very long. I didn't have to eliminate every friend or change all of my friendships to stay sober – I figure that's because I was the biggest drunk out of all of them. I found out that I had *REAL* friends – my friends respected what I was undertaking. I believe that you eventually need to go out and face the fact that drinking is part of our world and will be part of other people's lives. Once you are in a position of self-control and power you will be able to go out and live a normal life and it will further build your strength. I know, easier said than done.

Change your friends: The hardest decisions in my life were not which stock I should buy, should I change careers, what school should I attend, or a myriad of other dilemmas that we all face during our lives. The hardest decision has always been which relationships should I end and which should I nurture? For better or worse, it is your friendships and relationships that influence how your life turns out. It's easy to end a friendship or relationship when YOU get dumped. I should know, I've been dumped by plenty of people. It's sometimes difficult to determine if a friendship/relationship is good for you or not. I've also been in the position of having harmful relationships that I knew I should get out of, but for whatever reason I didn't want to. If you are serious about living sober you will probably have to end some friendships and relationships. You will also have to be very selective of the friendships you engage in moving forward.

Some of your *friends* may not want to hang out with you anymore, and you may find that you don't want to hang out with them anymore. They may act differently around you, feel nervous around you. Some will become fearful of you because they can sense the personal power you posses – which makes some people jealous and hateful towards you. Revel in knowing that you are powerful and can control yourself. Be ready for the brutal truth that some friendships and relationships may completely fall apart when you sober up, while other relationships will become deeper, stronger, healthier and more emotionally intimate. This is when

103

you will find out who your friends really are, what they are made of, and how much you can count on them. You will also find out what kind of friend you are to other people. If your friends don't want to help you, it may be because this friendship was based purely on alcohol. You may also find out that you are a big ass-hole and you were never a good friend to anyone anyway. If that's the case, you may want to learn how to be a better friend yourself.

Sooner or later challenges and problems will invade your life and your mind. You had to face the reality that you are a drunk, so face the reality that rough times will come and you will be tempted to give in and drink. Be prepared for these hard times, because they WILL come. That is when you will need your own strength, your friends and techniques for controlling your own thoughts. Have a friend or family member prepared and willing to talk you through these hard times.

Creating your own support group: Some people rely on AA as their support group (my experiences and thoughts on AA are in the next chapter). I found that it has been more beneficial for me to develop my own support group. My support group is personalized, consisting of only a few close friends and certain family members that understand me and my life goals. They know my drinking history, idiosyncrasies, character, strengths and weaknesses. I can't bullshit them – they know me all too well. (I found it too easy to bullshit anonymous groups – telling them only what I want them to hear).

My support group helps unknowingly bolster my willpower and strength. The strength I am referring to here is gained through their love and sincere support and my obligation to not let them down – they hold me accountable for my actions. I'm not talking about *tough love* when I say that they hold me responsible for my actions, I'm talking about the way people have become involved with my recovery by being available to talk with them, spending time with them and helping me stay sober during periods of temptation to drink. My group expects me to live up to my promises. You need to develop your own circle of friends and acquaintances to hang out with. These should be positive people that understand your dilemma and are determined to help you stay sober. (I will explain how to develop and use a Secret Support Group in chapter 12.)

Once you have made a promise to a friend, you need to stick to your word. Don't just stay sober for yourself; stay sober for the people you made promises to. You might have a friend that opens their home up to you and gives you a place to hang out when you know you're going to want to drink. Don't just leech the love and support out of these people, give something back to them. Take it upon yourself to ask them what you can do in return. Wash their car, help with house or yard chores, walk their dog, clean out the cat box – do something in return. If you don't give back to those that help you, eventually they're going to give up on you.

What if you don't have any friends? What if you are such a jerk that nobody likes you or cares about you? You may have burned so many bridges that you have no family or friends left to turn to. If that is your situation then this is where AA, a church group or religion can be invaluable. I want to pass along a cautionary warning about becoming too involved or dependant on a specific recovery group. I think that the whole "program" and "support group" philosophy can become a substitute addiction in itself. You cannot live only within your recovery group and become isolated from the rest of the world. You need to be a participant in life and you will have to learn how to live a life outside of these group associations. Many people also become overzealous in their new religion of sobriety. They can become so involved and obsessed with "the program" that *it* starts to run their lives.

Become selfish: You're going to be doing a lot of things that are completely selfish, but they will ultimately help you become a better person for other people to enjoy. This selfishness is different from the typical selfishness of egocentricity or being stingy. You want to be selfish in a good way, not in a mean or criminal way.

You must become self-centered about your own sobriety. If you feel that some people or places aren't good for you – then stay away from them. You need to always think about what's best for you, how you can keep yourself busy and keep getting stronger. Selfish also means that you think highly of yourself, you make sure that you get good food into your body, that you get enough rest, that you educate yourself, expand your mind and work on being a better friend to others. It is very important that you spend time reflecting on good things you have done in your life as well as think about, internalize and accept ownership for all the things you have fucked up in your life. Your mistakes are your own so be selfish with them too.

Relying on willpower: Most people think that willpower has to do with *stopping* something. But you use willpower in your life all the time. You use willpower to get up for work or school, go to a job you hate, mow the lawn, do laundry, clean your house, exercise, play a sport, make food – to make some of the simplest things in your life happen. You use willpower to accomplish most any goal, like furthering your education, looking for a job, starting a business, anything that you have ever been successful at accomplishing you used your own willpower.

Too many people are willing to believe in anything but themselves. You need to believe in yourself and your own willpower. It is easier than you might think to access your own willpower. The willpower is there, you just have to tell yourself and believe that it is yours to control and that you have more self-control than you have shown in the past. I had to sit and tell myself that I am strong enough to stay sober. This isn't some made-up, half-baked bullshit idea. If *you* don't tell yourself that you have the power, who else will? Maybe others have told you, but you didn't believe them – because you didn't believe in yourself. Then I suggest that you lie to yourself. So what. You lie to yourself about your drinking or drug problem. If you tell yourself the same lie often enough, you will start to believe it. Tell yourself, "I have the willpower, and screw anybody else that doesn't think I do."

106

The best way that I can explain how to develop internal strength and willpower is to allow your emotions to drive your thoughts. High self-esteem, love of oneself, love of others, your own ego and pride are some emotions you can use. Properly directed anger at yourself and others can build willpower. Muster up the willpower to show everyone else how strong you are. Maybe this sounds shallow or immature – so what? Use whatever works as long as it keeps you sober and it doesn't harm anyone else. You might be thinking, "This may have worked for you Mark, but I can't just tell myself that I have willpower and make it happen." Well if that is what you think, then you're right, you won't express and use your internal strength. You will be a drunk/addict until you really convince yourself that you do posses internal strength, willpower and the power to choose. When it comes to willpower, your attitude has to be – fake it until you make it.

Reward yourself. Remember that we are addicts, and we need to give ourselves a lot of short-term and immediate rewards. Do some math homework and figure out how much you spend on your habits – beer, wine, booze, cigarettes while drinking, etc. Then figure out how much you spend if you go to bars drinking. Make an honest accounting. Then start hiding the money you would have normally spent on these things and begin to reward yourself for staying sober. Buy nice things for yourself – clothes, shoes, haircut, a massage or day spa. Or buy gifts for people that you have always liked. Shopping and buying little gifts for people is one way of keeping your mind busy instead of just thinking about drinking. Buying gifts for someone else is a selfish gesture. You may be giving something away to someone else, but you will feel good about yourself. When buying gifts or spending money, be sure to spend less (about 50%) of what you would have normally spent on boozing. I recommend that you open a completely separate savings account where you put in $5.00 or $10.00 a day. Every day that I don't drink is another $10.00 towards my retirement, Christmas fund, dining out fund, etc. It's $10.00 towards anything other than drinking. (I will go into more detail in chapter 13.)

Do whatever you must: Addiction counselors and "Recovery Programs" have a list of things that you are supposed to NOT DO when you first stop drinking. I was told, "Don't make any major changes or decisions for the first year." Isn't quitting drinking a major change? "Don't get divorced, don't get married, don't change careers, don't move, don't buy a house, etc." This is great advice, but life and recovery are not neat and orderly. Life comes at us at unexpected speeds and from unforeseen directions. Life does not ask us what we want – nor do things always happen at convenient times – major changes are going to be an inevitable part of living sober.

Some things are out of your control and out of your hands. Some of these things HAVE to be done for you to get sober. You might have to move because of your financial situation. You might get a new job in a different city or be transferred. You might want to move because your roommate or neighbors are all drunks. You might find that divorce or separation is necessary if your spouse is abusive or unsupportive.

Some of the "don'ts" are an integral part of the sobering up process. You might be faced with having to make some of these decisions. Realize that your brain will be mush at first and your thinking may not be the clearest – which means you might not make the wisest decisions. Do the best you can to make the right decision, based on the knowledge you have at the time.

This takes me to another very sad aspect of living sober. If you are in a marriage or relationship and both of you are alcoholics, try to sober up together. If you do this alone, you may find yourself ALONE. The butt-ugly truth is that if you are the only one living sober, then the two of you will be going in different directions from one another. It is sad and difficult to accept, but you very well might have to leave your relationship. This is not always the case, but living in an alcoholic household while you're trying to lead a sober life doesn't give you much of a chance at success. Sometimes you just have to do what you have to do.

Personal experience: 30 days into my sobriety I was forced into a situation where I had to change careers. That was one of the first "don'ts" that I did. I went into a very high pressure and demanding career field – new car sales. To be successful at this job you have to work many hours, deal with heavy pressure from management to perform and handle rejection from customers all day long. This job required 55 to 60 hours per week. I would get up at 7:30a.m. to be at the dealership and ready for our daily sales meeting at 8:30a.m. Most of my day was then spent making follow-up calls or cold calling. I was allowed to take a break for lunch, but I never knew when customers would be coming in, so I didn't want to be gone for too long. My day eventually ended at 9:00p.m. If I was with a customer or they were still in the finance department I had to stay later. Twelve or more hours is a long time to work, but it kept my mind off drinking. I worked that 55 to 60 hours per week schedule for one year straight – no vacations or sick days. I undertook a lot of changes and tough projects that I was supposed to "NOT DO." I quit drinking, I went after a new career, I was trying to repair my marriage (I ended up being dumped by my wife anyway), and I was trying to change myself so I could become a better person. I moved out of our marital home and was divorced – all within the first year after I quit drinking.

Prepare for changes: Your brain is the organ which keeps the rest of your body running, tells you when to breath, what muscles to move, etc. Your mind and your thinking are also functions of the brain. When this organ (the brain) has alcohol flowing through it, it physically functions differently which causes your mind to interpret stimuli and data differently than it normally would. Your brain will become accustomed to functioning with a daily diet of alcohol and after an extended period of time, your brain only knows how to function with alcohol present. When you suddenly stop giving this organ alcohol, it will physically change how it functions. This may result in changes in your heart rate, eating and sleeping habits, bowel functions, and how your mind interprets stimuli and data. So expect your body and your mind to struggle.

Life can actually get a bit harder on many levels when you first sober up. Accept the fact that you are going to have some tough times and you may not be very pleasant to be around. Your body will be responding with changes (and not always for the best) and your mind is going to be racing – you won't be thinking clearly. Ask for a bit of understanding and patience from the people that are helping you. This isn't a license for you to be a jerk or to not care how you act, dress or what you say. You're trying to make a better life for yourself, but it will seem like nothing changes or happens fast enough. That's because your brain is all fucked up and it will take time for it to get used to functioning without the anesthesia known as alcohol.

You will be irritable, oversensitive and argumentative. (I would have argued with a fencepost if I thought it was in my way.) The smallest things will piss you off. You will have a short fuse and you will probably lash out at people for no obvious reason. Keep this in mind and keep your mouth shut. It's better to be quiet than to be argumentative. If you stumble and argue, apologize quickly and start over. This is a perfect time to learn how to treat people with kindness and consideration. Consciously work on being patient with people and yourself. I'm not saying that you should allow people to walk all over you. Pick your battles wisely – ask yourself, "Is this worth arguing over? Is this jack-off even worth arguing with?"

You will most likely be jealous of people who drink, which may turn into anger. Too bad – that's your problem not theirs. Let them do what they want, just worry about yourself. If it bothers you to be around people who drink, then change who you hang out with, or change your attitude about your friends that still drink. When you see others getting drunk, reflect and think to yourself, "was this how I acted?"

People will treat you differently. This will be because of how you are acting and treating them. You might be reacting in an

110

irritable fashion and not even realize it. Go slow – think before you speak. Don't get angry with friends and family. It's not their fault that your life feels like it's all fucked up. This is so important that I will repeat it again: **Think before you speak**. Think before you react or make decisions. You made bad decisions as a drunk, just because you're sober doesn't mean you'll make brilliant decisions now. This is a whole new experience for you and your brain. Don't expect every decision you make to be the right one. However, when you're sober, you can think things out better. If you make a bad decision or fuck something up, accept personal responsibility, find out if you can fix or remedy the situation, then move forward. Go slow – Stop – Think.

Physical changes: You will encounter some physical changes as well. You will probably lose weight. This initially will be due to fewer calories being taken in from drinking alcohol but it may be because of a loss of appetite. You will lack energy and enthusiasm. Your mind might want to do things but your body won't, so you will have to force yourself to eat healthy and stay physically active. You don't have to become a gym rat, but you need to keep your body moving. Go for walks or get involved in a group sport such as pickup basketball, softball or golf (walk don't ride). If you can afford it, join a gym and participate in group exercise classes. Exercising will help improve your appetite and your ability to sleep soundly.

If you have been drinking on a regular basis for one year or more, not only is your brain accustomed to functioning with, it is dependent on it, and so is your body – you're *body* will crave alcohol. As your body craves alcohol, it may start to revolt against you. Shaking, sweating, headaches, blurred vision, vomiting, diarrhea, inability to sleep or a racing heart can be expected – sounds fun doesn't it?

D.T.s (delirium tremens) is a harsh reality that can occur during the first 30 days of sobering up. Not everyone will be overcome by D.T.s. Just be prepared for the possibility. D.T.s are a condition

111

that cannot be ignored because they can be life threatening. The risk of sudden heart attack is REAL. The symptoms can come on rapidly. Be ready and willing to go to a hospital E.R. if you start to experience intense bouts of any of the conditions described above. If you do go to a hospital, tell the staff about your drinking history. This way they will know what your body is going through and they'll be able to stabilize you faster. You will most likely be put on an I.V. to replenish your body fluids and your heart will be monitored. Chances are good that you will be released within one day.

Personal experience: I still remember vividly what happened on my 21st day of sobriety. I woke up and it started out just like any other day, but for some reason, something seemed different. My brain finally told my body that this was it; I'll never be drinking again. "What??? Wait a fucking minute," is what my body said. "Oh no you don't. You fed me alcohol for 30 years and now you're not going to ever give it to me again? Fuck you! I'll get even with you asshole!" When my brain and body accepted that I would never drink again all hell broke loose – that is when I went into D.T.s. I began to sweat and shake. My mind exploded into multiple racing thoughts. Sweat began pouring out of me even more – I was freezing and soaking wet all at the same time. I became dizzy and I fell out of the kitchen chair. I walked to my living room, holding countertops, walls, furniture, whatever I could grab so I wouldn't fall over. I laid down on the sofa. I became violently ill. My stomach wanted no part of me. I threw up everything I had in me. After hours of puking and lying on the bathroom floor, I decided I had better try eating. My throat couldn't even squeeze cottage cheese down so I tried drinking some milk but I threw up anything that went in me. After I had thrown up everything else I started puking up stomach fluids. Once that was all gone I threw up blood. I laid on the bathroom floor, sweating, crying, shaking, shitting in the toilet, and then throwing up in it.

My wife came home later that night, after she had been riding her horse and drinking with her friends at the barn. She is a registered nurse and knew immediately what was happening to me. "Mark, you're going through D.T.s. Have a beer to take the edge off." I looked at her in disbelief and asked, "Are you trying to fucking kill me?" "Your body needs alcohol, just have one beer to take the edge off, just have a drink." I don't fault her for telling me this. She truly wasn't trying to harm me, kill me or get me to start drinking again. I can't be mad at her for telling me to do something that she thought would help me feel better. However, that one beer would have sent me right back to drinking again. If one helped me feel good, then two would make me feel better and on and on.

I would not wish what I went through on my worst enemy. I have experienced a lot of physical pain in my life, but without exaggeration, going through D.T.s was the worst pain I have ever felt.

Turning to God: My goal in this section is not to persuade for or against any religious belief system, nor to debate the existence or nonexistence of a God or Deity. But I can't caution enough that during the initial sobering up time (30-90 days) you will be vulnerable to being influenced into spiritual beliefs. Many people will tell you, "All you need to do is turn to God" or "Let go and let God" or "You HAVE to accept a higher power." Look, if you're not a believer in God – then don't suddenly start now – hoping that God will cure you. If you do that, you are just setting yourself up for a big letdown. God isn't going to cure you, I can't cure you – only YOU can cure you.

Many people believe that God will give them signs along the way. If this is your belief system – great – watch very closely for those signs from God. But God is only going to do so much – most of this will be up to you. If you have a strong religious foundation, then use it to your own empowerment with sobriety. If you are a believer, you probably already know how to turn to God. Your God and your religion's teachings will give you something to turn to in times of trouble and temptation. You may want to consider delving deeper into your faith and becoming more active with its

113

mission. If you have fallen away from your faith, this can be a perfect time to revisit it and get to know your God again. Most religious groups offer "Alcohol Free" get-togethers and support groups. Become a participant and actively celebrate your faith.

You cannot always burden your friends with your need to talk. There may be times when it's too late at night, or simply no one is available. You will need to start relying on your own strength. That's when you might want to try turning to God or learning about spirituality. But again I want to issue a warning of caution about becoming too religiously overzealous. It's easy to use religion as a substitute addiction and become obsessed with it. You don't want to be the person that everyone hides from because all you talk about is how God helped with your recovery. I would never chide anyone about their religious beliefs nor would I ever try to talk anyone OUT of their faith. But if you don't have a legitimately strong faith, you can't suddenly turn religious and expect God to keep you sober. A Minister once told me, "It's pretty easy to find Jesus in prison, but when you get out He's nowhere to be found." I believe the same can happen with recovering addicts. We find God for a short time when we first sober up, then forget all about Her if we relapse or go back to our old habits. If you are so moved, slowly learn how to pray and get to know a God. After six months, then join a church, synagogue, mosque or whatever your religion of choice is. Choose a religion when you are ready and then stick with it. Never expect or think that it's up to God, your spouse, partner, friend, family or boss to sober you up. You are in charge of yourself and sobriety is completely up to you.

I have heard other drunks say, "God doesn't want me to live this way." Here is my own belief: God allows and wants you to live any way you want. God does not meddle in the personal affairs and doings of his followers or dissenters. A fair and loving God does not show favoritism. God makes sure that the universe and nature keeps functioning. This is evidenced to me by the fact that even people who don't believe in God or follow a certain religion can

114

still live fulfilling, moral lives. A God should be turned to for spiritual, emotional, social and moral guidance. I do not expect God to do my work for me or give me anything that She would not give to anyone else.

Personal experience: I talked with God a lot when I first dried out. I had nothing else to turn to, so I trusted that there was a God. I spent my first three months of sobriety attending Lutheran services every Sunday. It always seemed like I would get a little nugget of inspiration out of going to church, but I would leave more upset than when I got there. I would listen to the minister say, "God loves you" and how "We should all try to be forgiving." Then I would think of my wife who was at home sleeping off a hangover after going out nightclubbing with her girlfriends, coming home with other men's phone numbers. I didn't think God really cared about me.

I also spent a lot of time reading the *Life Recovery Bible*. The *Life Recovery Bible* is a great book with translations into modern language explaining how the stories are pertinent and relatable to our current lifestyles. Some parts still require you to rely on pure faith. Answers like, "Because God loves you," and "That's why Jesus died on the cross for you," didn't help me want to stay sober or accept the way my life was going. These statements actually just raised more questions and then I had even more skeptical thoughts about God. After a while I began getting angry at God but I knew that being angry would be counter-productive, so I started *praying to* and *talking with* my deceased mother's spirit – which I still do. This might be where I drew some of my willpower from. My mother never lets me down.

When I was close to my one year sobriety anniversary I was having a very bad period. I was crying a lot and had too many racing thoughts and mental anguish. One day I was sitting on my kitchen floor crying and I just couldn't take it anymore. I stood up, walked over to my living room window and stared out. I said, "Okay God, if you're there, I will give you my pain. You can have it." I felt a strange sense of relief and a small amount of calm. I had no dramatic, miraculous event take place. My life still sucked from my perspective. I still felt the desire to get drunk, I still didn't have the woman I loved back, I was still depressed, but I gave my pain away. Is there a God and did She take my pain and bear it for me? I don't know and I don't care. All I know is that this worked to help me feel better *at that time*. I'm sure that all I did was talk myself into letting go of my pain and my mind cooperated.

God, the Bible and church was a big struggle for me but I did my best to accept and simply enjoy with an open mind. Attending mass and reading the *Life Recovery Bible* served a purpose for me at the appropriate time. I still have a hard time blindly accepting organized religion's teachings. However I do see calmness and happiness in the faces of people that do have faith. I wish I could have that. I wish I could be able to know inside that God cares for me and that She has a master plan – I just think She's a bit too busy to worry about me.

As you go through the sobering up process you will find that there are a lot of other recovered/recovering people out there in the same boat as you – you are not alone. You will realize that others can live normal lives as sober people. Get to know these people better. Talk with them about how they cope with living sober. Find out how they bring pleasure and fun into their lives. Learn from their successes and failures. Most important – believe in yourself.

#11) Is AA for you?

What works for me may not work for you.

I want to open this chapter with the disclaimer that this is not an AA bashing session. My own experiences with AA have not been rewarding for me. These are my personal opinions. I am not going to speak ill of AA. I respect AA along with its ideals. AA has clearly been of help to millions of individuals since its inception. The 12-step program is a great idea and it may be the system that works for you. But getting sober and staying that way is still going to be up to you.

A brief history of AA. In early 1935 AA unofficially began in Akron, OH. Two men began an approach towards treating alcoholics that had never been tried before. In the fall of 1935, one of these men moved to New York, NY. and the first AA group had actually been formed. In 1937, a second group started in New York as well as another group in Cleveland, OH. In 1939 the first AA publication appeared. In 1976 AA had an estimated membership of more than two million. In 2005, AA was composed of over 105,000 groups in approximately 150 countries.

The philosophy of AA was pure and altruistic when it was started. AA does not claim that they will sober you up or keep you sober. AA offers fellowship and a program that alcoholics can follow. AA philosophy does not assert that you must follow every step to the letter and attend meetings every day – it is the people involved with it that made these claims to me. When I attended meetings, I was constantly reminded, "You can't do this on your own... you have to follow the steps... you must accept a higher power... you *have* to attend meetings every day for the first 90 days... etc." Call me a heretic – but that's bullshit. It sounds good but it isn't real – real life doesn't always allow a person to attend meetings every day, fulfill every step or even want to follow every step.

I'm sure I'll get plenty of hate mail about this, but I find it difficult to listen to the rhetoric I hear from many members. Examples of rhetoric come when I asked, "How do I deal with the anger I feel? How can I control my urges to drink out of spite?" The standard answer would be, "You have to work the steps," or "The answers are in the *Big Book*." That isn't an answer, that's brainwashed rhetoric.

The problem I have is that many AA *members* insist that you have to follow every step (at least that's how it was at the meetings I attended). I didn't follow the steps in order, I didn't follow or fulfill every step, I never had a sponsor, I didn't attend meetings on a regular basis. I relied on my own willpower and I will continue to do so to stay sober.

AA is not a religious organization, but I personally have a hard time accepting the steps involving a "higher power" and accepting a God or believing that a God will take away my problems. My problems are mine and I had better take full responsibility for them and my actions. I understand that many drunks are weak when first sobering up – searching for any help they can get – and sometimes believing in a God is all you have to help you.

As a recovered drunk myself, I am aware of how vulnerable and impressionable we are when we first sober up. Don't become a lemming and just follow the crowd or become so emotionally invested in "the program" that *it* becomes your new addiction. Also be wary of falling prey to any religious group that you might not truly believe in.

While I was in the early stages of sobering up, I thought I would try the AA steps. Some of the steps were helpful for me to grow into a better person, but they didn't help me to control my urge to drink. I used the 12-step outline to set up my own personalized game plan. It wasn't as much of a game plan as it was goals – followed by a list of specific activities that I needed to do to accomplish those goals. The written plan which I customized for myself gave me a point of reference to go back to whenever I didn't know what to do with my time or when I had feelings that sobering up wasn't worth the effort.

I personally believe in only one of the steps, the first. The other 11 steps won't get you sober, won't keep you sober – or I should say they didn't help *me* stay sober. A few of the steps did help me look within myself and address some of my own personal issues. However none of these issues had anything to do with the fact that I am an alcoholic. I would get drunk because I liked getting drunk and used alcohol as an escape from reality.

Step #1 - "We admitted we were powerless over alcohol – that our lives had become unmanageable." This is the one step that can help in sobriety. Admit that you're a drunk and that you need to do something about it. My *body* may be powerless over alcohol but I am not powerless over alcohol. I know that it is my choice to self-introduce alcohol into my bloodstream. Once it is in my system I cannot control how much my body wants. So I exert power over alcohol by consciously not putting it in to my system.

Step #2 - "Came to believe that a Power greater than ourselves could restore us to sanity." No, I don't believe that. I accept that if I am **not** going to drink it will be up to ME and nobody else. If I am going to be a better person, that is also my own responsibility – not some invisible power's or a deity's.

Step #3 - "Made a decision to turn our will and our lives over to the care of God *as we understood Him*." Sorry but this just doesn't work for me. I am not going to turn my will and my life over to

119

anything or anyone. I accept that I am solely responsible for my own thoughts and actions – be they good or bad. I can follow the rules of a denomination if that's what I believe I should do and I can worship a God if I want. But ultimately I am responsible for governing myself.

Step #4 - "Made a searching and fearless moral inventory of ourselves." (This is good advice for any adult, whether you're an addict or not.) I worked pretty heavily on this step. I made my list of all the personal flaws and quirks that I thought I had. I wanted to honestly understand what was holding me back from having better relationships and achieving all the things I felt I could in life. I wanted to accept personal responsibility for all the things I had been doing wrong and what areas of my personality that I could improve. This step helped me realize that it wasn't *only* drinking that was holding me back but it was ME – my laziness and my own willingness to be more productive.

Step #5 - "Admitted to God, to ourselves and to another human being the exact nature of our wrongs." Admitting my flaws to myself was easy – I like me and I don't think I'm that bad of a guy. But the day I wanted to talk to God about this, She called in sick. So I decided to bore my two best buddies, Jeff and Mike with my list of personal defects and flaws. They were extremely impressed by my honest reflection. They agreed with me on some points where I felt I had been acting like a despicable piece of crap as a human being. They disagreed on others and felt I was being too hard on myself. I am glad I did this step. I think it allowed me to get closer to myself and closer to them. I still have this list – I review it annually. It's nice to see that I have fixed some of my defects, but I still think I'm a despicable piece of crap as a human being – but I'm sober.

Step #6 - "Were entirely ready to have God remove all these defects of character." I understand this principle – allow someone else to help free you of your flaws and have them bear your burdens with you. Why should God remove these? I should be willing to act responsibly and address these defects myself.

Step #7 - "Humbly asked Him to remove our shortcomings." I feel that I should be the one to consciously remove my own defects. I am responsible and accountable for my own flaws. It is up to me to free myself of them. (And why is God always a gender specific Him? Anybody ever consider maybe God is a Her? Or maybe neither?)

Step #8 - "Made a list of all the persons we had harmed, and became willing to make amends to them all." Making this list was easy – it was everyone I had ever known (except for me, I had always been nice to myself). Seriously, I made my list of people that I felt I should make amends to. Some of these people I felt that all I needed to do was apologize to them but I didn't feel that I needed to make amends with them. As I have stated, there are plenty of people who turned against me and undermined me when I stopped drinking. I feel no sense of obligation to them and I don't want them in my life anymore. I don't feel like I need to be willing to make amends or apologize to them.

Step #9 - "Made direct amends to such people wherever possible, except when to do so would injure them or others." (The last part of this step means that you shouldn't go to the neighbor and say, "sorry that I banged yer 'ol lady when you were out of town," – keep shit like that to yourself, it won't do anybody any good.) I made my list of people that I felt I had harmed and sought them out so I could apologize and make amends with them. For me, making amends and living amends are two distinctly different acts. I can make amends by repaying a debt, be it financial or otherwise. Once the debt has been paid, my amends are done. With some people, all I did was apologize – no amends. I said, "I'm sorry," I made my peace and now they can go fuck themselves – I never want to see them or hear from them again.

Living my amends is expressed towards the people that I care about. This means that I will treat the other person better than I

121

may have treated them in the past. I pay attention to them, show respect by listening, appreciate them, try to understand their point of view better, be available to help them whenever and however I can.

As I made the rounds to serve my apologies and make amends I was surprised at what I heard. "You're an alcoholic? Well you're the most productive and successful alcoholic I ever met. No, you never insulted me or my wife. Oh sure, you would get a bit too drunk once in a while, but you were never belligerent or annoying. Hell, I could always count on you if I needed help with anything. So you quit drinking huh? Let's have a beer to celebrate."

Step #10 - "Continued to take personal inventory and when we were wrong promptly admitted it." When I first stopped drinking I was irritable and argumentative for no apparent reason and this was a principle that I needed to pay close attention to. If you argue or get shitty with someone, be ready and willing to say, "I'm sorry, I was wrong." To me this is basic common sense and it is something that mature individuals do all the time, regardless of whether they are recovering alcoholics or not.

Step #11 - "Sought through prayer and meditation to improve our conscious contact with God, *as we understood Him*, praying only for knowledge of His will for us and the power to carry that out." Ummm, what about my will and the fact that I am solely responsible for my own actions? Nothing wrong with being introspective, thinking, praying and meditating to find guidance and answers. This is helpful when you have a desire to do the right things, treat people with civility and make better decisions. I meditate to my mother's spirit. Maybe God talks to me through her?

Step #12 - "Having had a spiritual awakening as a result of these steps, we tried to carry this message to alcoholics, and to practice these principles in all our affairs." This whole step rubs me wrong. I had no "spiritual awakening" (I don't think God likes me

122

anyway). I came to my own conclusions on the benefits of sobriety. I honestly accept the good and bad consequences of my actions. You can call it an "awakening" but this came only after I was physically cleared of alcohol.

I understand that this principle states that we should carry the message to other alcoholics. What message? That they should become a member of a recovery group or embrace my sober way of life? I will not force my philosophy or my way of life upon anyone. If someone wants to talk with me about alcoholism I will do so, if someone wants my help, I will always offer it, otherwise I mind my own business.

The best way that I can carry the message is to live sober. I *don't preach* – I *teach* by example. True, I wrote this book and I run **www.LivingSoberSucks.com** but these are intended for those who are actively seeking help. I don't go around lecturing people on the ills of alcoholism. I want to be a welcome guest wherever I go. I let people do what they want and let them get as drunk as they want. If their drinking bothers me, then I don't hang out with them. I worry about myself and just live sober. If someone wants to have what I have in life, I can tell them or show them by example. Your turn to carry the message and help others may come. Just by allowing others to see you living sober may be more of an inspiration to them than you realize.

If you want to become a nicer person, then recovering requires controlling yourself, self-forgiveness and asking others for their forgiveness. No shallow "I'm sorry" and then you continue life as it always was. You will need to change how you approach difficulties and how you treat people. If you want to learn useful principles on how to be a better person and better communicator every day of your life, I suggest you read Dale Carnegie *"How to Win Friends and Influence People."*

The development of this book began in 1912 while Dale Carnegie was teaching business courses, and it was published three years *before* the first AA publication was printed. I have a far better understanding and a much higher appreciation for Dale Carnegie's book now that I am sober. I remember when a good friend of mine gave me this book as a gift. I was a younger, angrier man when I received it (about 25 years ago). This book has positively influenced my life more than any other book I have ever read. It opened my eyes to genuinely appreciating other people, being more accepting and open-minded with other people and truly trying to be of help to others. This book also reminds me that my attitude and my actions fall solely and squarely on my shoulders – that my life is in fact a result of my own doing. Dale Carnegie's books have helped me become a balanced person. His books may not offer techniques on how to sober up, but he offers a lot of principles on how to be a better person once you *have* sobered up. I read through my dog-eared and highlighted hardcover copy at least once a year.

I would also like to make the assertion that changing your personal flaws for the better is not a requisite of living sober. Most recovery programs contend that you have to change how you treat people, repair your personal flaws and be part of a support group in order to live sober. It is my belief that you don't have to change your character or become a nicer person to live sober. This is often referred to as being a "dry drunk," which simply means that you no longer drink but you still exhibit poor behavior as a person. So what – as long as you are sober. You can be an asshole all you want – nobody will like you – but you can still live a sober life.

Also, **all drunks are not jerks** and all members of a recovery program are not saints. Maybe your biggest flaw is that you simply drink too much. Maybe the only person you have harmed is you. Reflection, introspection and the pursuit of self-improvement is healthy, but don't be too hard on yourself.

The "Higher Power" illusion: Have you considered that a great Higher Power could be you – and your own ability to control yourself? What a feeling of pride, power and accomplishment it is to know that you sobered up on your own personal strength. You might be weak and your life is out of control, but a Higher Power cannot stop you from drinking; only *you* can stop you from drinking. Don't just blindly buy into the external "Higher Power" proposition and the "12-steps are the only answer" thesis. Try being your own internal Higher Power, try doing this on your own. If you fail you can always seek fellowship. But when you do succeed on your own you will feel a sense of pride, power and reward like nothing else. Birds and butterflies won't be following you around, but you will feel pretty damn good about yourself. You CAN become and stay sober using your own willpower. It won't be easy. There is no easy method. It takes effort and self-discipline to stay sober. You have the willpower!

In support of Alcoholics Anonymous: Now that I have spewed all my negatives, I would like to say some positive things about AA and their fellowship. Clearly, Alcoholics Anonymous is popular and is of benefit to many members. I think it's a good idea to attend a few meetings. It's good to hear from other drunks because you won't feel as if you're the only one in the world with this problem. Go to a couple of different locations so you can hear from all social levels. At AA gatherings you will meet a wide spectrum of personalities, social backgrounds, races, and hear hundreds even thousands of different stories of drunkenness. Some stories are funny, some are so very sad. You'll hear from people that are far worse off than you, you'll hear from people who are nowhere near as bad as you are. You will hear stories of success and stories of failure. You will no doubt hear some inspiring words, techniques or ways of thinking so you can get yourself sober and stay sober. You just might find that the fellowship your AA group offers is perfect for you.

AA might be helpful for you if you're single and are accustomed to hanging out in the bar atmosphere – some AA locations offer that type of environment. Maybe you just moved to a new city and you're all alone, maybe you don't have a circle of family and good friends. Then AA might be a great place for you to hang out.

If you want to live sober I think you should have as much information about recovery, addiction, and other people's personal experiences as possible. You don't have to believe everything you read or hear about recovery. Make your own choices, ask a lot of questions. Determine which techniques will work best for you.

With that said, I do recommend having a copy of *"The 12 Steps of AA."* I also suggest *"12 Steps"* and *"Living Sober."* The AA steps are very proactive and require you to reflect on yourself and take responsibility for your life. You might find that following the steps to the letter and being active with AA is the best thing for you. I believe that you can use the steps as a reference guide – pick and choose the steps that you think you need or that will benefit you the most. I think that it's okay to do the steps out of sequence. I also believe that you need to dissect each step and consider doing them in a fashion that fits your personality and belief system. Don't avoid the steps that require you to think and write, those may be the most beneficial for you.

At this stage you might be thinking that if I'm recommending the 12 AA steps, why can't you just go to AA meetings, follow their program and you'll be cured? It won't work that way. AA doesn't claim that they can cure you, only *you* can cure *you*. Sobering up is a solitary project done by you alone. You may have support but it is done with your own willpower and the acceptance that you have a choice.

My bottom line is that I don't think "the program" should become the focus of your life. Eventually you will have to go to work, school, parties, social events or someplace other than a meeting. You want to be fully engaged in every joy life offers you – and you can do it sober.

#12) Life after liquor

Okay I'm sober, what's next?

Staying sober is not a onetime event, it is an ongoing, daily project that requires patience. As long as you can be patient with yourself, then I'm sure your friends and family will be patient with you too. It will take time to see the improvements and benefits. After a month, three months, six months, a year, two years, etc., it all starts paying off. I'm not making any false promises to you. This **will** take time, it will be tough on occasion, things may not always go as planned. Some things will get better, I can promise you that.

Time lines: The longer you stay sober the easier some things will become. On the flip side, some things will get harder. If you have been drinking on a regular basis for a year or more, your brain has acclimated itself to functioning under the influence of alcohol. When you stop feeding your brain alcohol it may not function as well as you would like it to. There are time frames that will pass where changes will occur. 30 days, 90 days and one year. From my own experience, I can tell you that it will take almost 90 days of sobriety for your brain to heal and start functioning normal again. It will probably take up to one year of sobriety for your brain, body and mind to work together in sober unison. You may not notice these changes because they happen very subtly. I suggest that you spend time reflecting and thinking about your progress on these anniversary dates and you will hopefully notice and acknowledge the changes that have been taking place.

Over the first 30 days you will most likely encounter periods of confusion and irritability. You might also experience the *Pink Cloud*. The pink cloud is a feeling that everything is going great and you feel wonderful. You don't wake up with a hangover headache and everything seems to be going smoothly. You have jumped back into performing normal activities with full enthusiasm and you feel full of energy and excitement. Your new sobriety makes you wonder, "Why didn't I do this sooner? I am so excited that I want to do everything all at once." Then reality hits – some adversity or catastrophe strikes. You think, "I thought quitting drinking would eliminate all my problems. Why is this problem happening?" In the past, you would have addressed or avoided problems by drinking. Now you have to face this situation sober. Confusion and anger overtake you. You haven't had to deal with problems sober before, "How am I going to handle this?"

Now is when you need to stop, breathe and think. Remind yourself that drinking will NOT help solve this problem. Your mind is not accustomed to handling stress sober. Your best option may be to do nothing. That's right – NOTHING. Try to defer the problem so you can address it at a later date. Not making a decision can be a decision in itself. I understand that some problems and decisions cannot be deferred and require immediate action. In that case, breathe deep, think them over slowly and remind yourself that drinking will NOT help you make a better decision or make this problem go away. Then address the problem or make the decision, based on the best knowledge that you have at that time. You might make the wrong decision, but it will be better than making a drunken decision.

At around 90 days sober your mind and body will be more comfortable with each other. You should be less irritable and the act of *not drinking* should be becoming a natural feeling for you. (You should have saved up $900.00 by now. You will learn how to do this in Chapter #13.) At 90 days you will also notice that you are becoming less obsessed with talking about recovery and alcohol. Hopefully your conversations will be focused on life's daily events. Your interactions with your spouse, partner, children and friends should be stabilizing, less tension riddled and emotionally explosive. (More on the drinking spouse/partner relationship later in this chapter.)

As you approach 90 days sober, the temptation to drink may start to resurface. You will think, "I made it this long, I could have one drink." **Don't do it**. You will go right back to drinking as much as you used to and you will have to start this all over again. I personally know that if I take one drink, one snort or one drag off a cigarette, I'll be right back to my junk again. All of the "addicts" that I know will agree with me. Once we're hooked on our junk, we can't toy with it on a social or recreational level.

It will take close to one year for all of your efforts to really start paying off. Your mind will be sharper and your emotions should be more stable. You might be saying, "One year! Holy shit I can't wait that long." One year is nothing – we're talking about being healthy, stable and **sober for the rest of your life**. Remember that staying sober is not a onetime event; it is a goal that you will work at every day for the rest of your life.

After a year of sobriety you will be in a better position mentally and emotionally to slow down your hectic schedule. Remember that I told you to stay busy and work as much as you can? Now will be the time to ease into relaxation. I'm not talking about becoming lazy – this relaxation has to do with your mind, body and soul. Relaxation will help you have a calmer approach towards accepting life. I suggest that you spend some time to do absolutely nothing. That's right, sit and stare out the window, lay back on the couch with your eyes closed. Spend an hour occasionally being completely still. Spend this time reflecting on all that you have done and accomplished. Meditate, pray, reaffirm your decision to live sober, think about the people that have helped you along the way – feel a sense of love and gratitude towards them. Relax and feel good about yourself – bask in your own personal strength.

Don't get me wrong, life will not become some happy panacea of peace and joy. There will still be problems. Things will still go wrong. You will still get angry and argue. People will not do what they said they will do and shit will still happen. Mind and soul relaxation will help you control your urges to drink when things do go wrong, which they inevitably will. You won't have to resort to drinking to avoid problems – you will be able to relax your mind and think your problems through.

How do I get rid of all my guilt? "I want to free myself of all the remorse, the regrets, the wreckage, the damage I've done. I want to eliminate the pain – I want to pay my penance and clear the slate." I understand that it is natural to want to rid oneself of painful emotions. To make restitution to those you have wronged and make everything better again. Sorry to tell you this, but sometimes you can't rid of these things – and who (or what) do you want to give this wreckage to anyway? Some things in life can't be undone. That doesn't mean that you have to live the rest of your life with guilt and sadness.

You can free yourself of these feelings by accepting the reality that you are personally responsible for past actions. But the good part is you do not have to be controlled by past actions or past experiences. You want to learn from them and learn to not repeat them. As you live sober, you don't have to react in the ways you once did to situations because you won't be hiding inside of a bottle. For example, you don't have to argue or get into fights with people; you don't have to get involved in dangerous, risky or unhealthy activities. You won't ignore bills, problems or conflicts. You will address your problems head-on and they won't get out of your control.

If you feel as if you need to pay some sort of penance, the best way will be for you to live a sober and fulfilling life. Live happy and healthy for your partner, your children, your friends and yourself. Your penance may also include that you pay off your debts, pay child support, serve jail time or community service.

Extend the olive branch and ask the people that are important to you what penance they would like of you. What can you do for *them* to clear your relationship? You don't have to do this with everyone. I believe that some things are better left unaddressed. Some people aren't worth the time and effort to make amends with. Some situations may be too painful to revisit – why open up old wounds? Again I will clarify that you shouldn't live in denial or hide from your past – some things in life cannot be undone – but you do not have to live and act based on what you have done or what has happened in your past. These things are only past experiences – and that's all they are.

The best way to *not* be controlled by your past is to *not* constantly re-live it. Don't keep thinking about it and don't tell everyone you meet your history. Retelling your history will only remind you of it and replaying bad scenes from your life will not allow you to love yourself, love others and constructively move forward with your life. It is true that some of your past actions can't be undone. There may be factual conditions that must be dealt with – unplanned children, car accidents, fights, wasted money, ruined relationships, broken marriages, criminal records. Accepting responsibility and dealing with things that have happened can be your penance.

Your mind will believe almost anything you tell it. If you keep telling yourself that you are a drunk, a loser or a failure – your mind will help you fulfill these thoughts through your actions. Instead of thinking about the past, I want you to visualize future successful experiences. This will direct your new thoughts and actions. The best technique that has worked for me is to tell myself how great of a person I *can* be. I try not to use negative words in my self-affirmations. For example, instead of saying, "I am not a loser," I will use positive statements like, "I **am** successful at what I do. I **am** a good friend. I **have** control over alcohol." This is not just using positive thinking. I make sure that I visualize myself having *realistic* successful experiences with friends, in business, with family members, in my life. I see myself living a normal, happy life sober. I dream these thoughts, I even daydream these thoughts. Repetition of these visions will override past bad experiences and enable my mind to see future good experiences. The more detailed successful visions I generate for myself, the more naturally positive thinking and successful actions come into my life.

Ridding yourself of guilt requires conscious, positive, forward thinking by you. You can't keep blaming your parents, society or the injustices of others for your present condition. Blaming someone else or yourself will not solve your present problem or improve your future. Past experiences explain how you got to where you are and why you feel like you do. Where you go and how you approach your future is your own choice. You can visualize and think of yourself as the helpless victim of past experiences or you can visualize and plan for your future.

I am only briefly touching on positive visualization. This technique and some of the other subjects that I will cover are far beyond the scope of this book. I want to pass along some basic ideas and exercises to help you maintain your sobriety. If there is a specific subject that you want to know more about, then read up on it. There are a lot of books available on these topics that illustrate techniques and mental exercises. A simple search of Amazon.com will be worth your time. Search phrases like, Positive Psychology, Ridding guilt, Self image or Self esteem.

Have Fun and be playful: Just because you no longer drink doesn't mean you can't have fun. You owe it to yourself to have a normal, active life. Being playful means that you allow yourself and others to act silly or try new things. New things could be learning a new dance step, going on a new ride, skating, going to the zoo, a comedy club or movie. Silly doesn't mean acting rude, boisterous, getting drunk or doing some other risky activity. It requires you to be willing to step away from your normal safety limits. It may include dangerous activities like skydiving, rock climbing, snowboarding, etc. Playfulness means that you are not serious all the time – smile once in a while. Let fun people and fun events happen without you being a wet blanket by telling others how not to act or what to do. If you don't like how others are acting or you think they are being too silly, then leave the environment. You have the choice.

A great way to bring fun into your life is to watch less TV. Go and do things, participate in a sport or a hobby you enjoy. Go to a gym, work in your yard, garden, go to baseball games, football games, carnivals, amusement parks. Go golf, swim, on picnics, to concerts, plays, movies, dancing, read more books,,, whatever. You don't have to drink to do these activities and you don't have to drink to make them fun.

Having fun does not mean pleasure seeking. It was the constant *pleasure seeking* that caused us to drink, and constant pleasure seeking is an un-winnable battle. Continuously pursuing fictitious and unrealistic pleasures will leave you feeling empty, so it is important to be realistic about what true happiness and pleasure is for you. Work on enjoying the things that you *do have* and that you *can do*. Relax your mind and enjoy the *now*. Redirect your thoughts away from the things that you think you are missing. Realize that you will always want more no matter how much you currently have.

Feelings definitely do influence actions and vice versa. Doing fun and playful activities will lift you to happier emotions. We all have emotional swings but you can still be happy even if you are in a blue mood. Acting happy will allow you to enjoy the present even if you are in a quiet or down mood. I am not saying that you should live in denial of your moods. I am not minimizing the reality of depression or trying to sound simplistic. Various mood swings are a natural part of life. Just don't allow the sour or down moods to control your actions. Every depressing emotion, feeling or thought does not have to be *reacted to* or *acted on*.

133

Psychological studies have shown that there is a flow or sequence of events that typically takes place that affects our happiness:

#1-Thoughts
#2-Feelings
#3-Actions

The things that we are *thinking* about (#1) causes us to have *feelings* (#2) and we *act* (#3) according to how we feel. Depression feeds off of this sequence. We *think* depressing thoughts – some of which are due to real problems but most are conjured up in our own mind – then we start to *feel* depressed. These feelings cause us to lack energy and enthusiasm, then we become inactive. This sequence starts to repeat itself and it snowballs into full blown depression. Emotions and feelings are real – but they are still just thoughts. Those thoughts, emotions and feelings start to control our conscious thinking, then we follow-up by acting on how we feel and how we are thinking. That's when "shit" becomes reality to us even when the "shit" doesn't even factually exist. "Shit" doesn't have to become reality.

One of the best strategies that have worked for me when I need to get out of funk is to take these three events and reverse the sequence. When I start thinking depressing thoughts about any aspect of drinking (past or present), I consciously say to myself, "Stop it, stop it." I will consciously make myself active. *Activity* causes my *thoughts* to stay focused on what I am doing, then I *feel* better that I am doing something or have accomplished something. This may sound hokey and homespun, but it has worked for me and for others. I am not saying that it makes reality, past events or problems disappear. But ultimately it DOES help me to feel better and feeling better helps control my thoughts into a creative direction. I am not hiding from my feelings, but I know that if I become active and stay active I will feel better and my thoughts will be constructive.

I start with simple productive activities. I'll do my dishes, wash laundry, clean up my house a bit, organize my books or desk. I also make lists of bigger projects that I want to get done. Or I might look at my list of life goals and start working on an activity that will bring me closer to accomplishing them. Like writing this book. If I didn't actively work on it, it would never have gotten done. I also make sure that I stay physically active. I walk my dogs, jog, run or go to the gym. Once I'm at the gym I start talking with people (about positive things). Do you have any hobbies, interests or sports that you like to participate in? Even doing these things alone is still positive action. Can you help a friend with some of their chores or projects? Force yourself to be active and allow happier feelings to come your way.

Here's an example of how thoughts (shit) become reality. A friend of mine ordered some food over the phone using her credit card. The food delivery never showed up and after an hour she called the sandwich shop to find out why. The store had already closed for the evening so there was no answer. She started getting all pissed off that they forgot to send her order. She worked herself up into an angry froth. Then she started thinking that the order taker must stolen her credit card number. As this worry intensified, she decided to call her credit card company and cancel her card. She wasted over an hour fidle-fuckin' around with the credit card company, then spent the rest of her night restless, angry, upset and filled with anxiety over, "Why did this happen to me?"

The next morning she called the sandwich shop to complain and accuse the employee of stealing her card number. The manager calmly explained that the credit card had been rejected as "nonexistent" and that is why she did not receive her order. The store had called her back and left a voicemail about this. Turns out that she never listened to her voicemail that night AND she had mixed up some of the credit card numbers she gave them. A simple explanation as to what had transpired and why she didn't get her sandwich.

My point is that all the shit she was worried about *didn't even exist*. She allowed her thoughts to create a fictitious problem for her and she was acting according to her thoughts. She was all upset and worried about things that never occurred. Her thoughts allowed her to think that the universe had "singled her out" to ruin her night – and it was ruined by her own conjured up anxiety – all over a stupid fucking sub sandwich. She was about a week into her sobriety when this happened. I mention this to point out the irrational thoughts you might encounter during the early stages of sobriety. To her credit she openly admits that she has learned a lot from this experience (and so have I). She has learned to not allow irrational thoughts to control her. She has learned to be patient and get all the facts before reacting. She has learned that her own imagination and thoughts really do control how she feels and acts.

Understanding and Accepting Boredom: I talk about how dull, boring and mundane life is as a sober person. While many aspects of my life seem mundane to me, it has nothing to do with sobriety. I have come to the realization that all alcohol did was create drama and chaos in my life – along with numbing my brain so mundane activities felt interesting and allowed hours to pass by – which gave me the impression that life was exciting. Chaos and drama is NOT excitement – that is called anxiety.

Yes, it's boring to pay bills – but I don't have the drama and anxiety of late fees and collection calls. It seems uneventful to have a conversation with a friend or lover about simple things – but I don't have the drama of tension filled confrontations over inane topics or having to apologize for a drunken argument. Laundry, house cleaning, grocery shopping – life – all *seem* mundane without alcohol.

All of those things felt more entertaining while drunk – but I was really never fully engaged doing those things drunk. For instance, notice how you can sit and talk to some other drunk for hours about stupid shit when you're drunk? But you would never spend five minutes talking with that person if you were sober.

(And good luck if you can remember what you even talked about with that person.) The reason is because you are never really fully engaged when you're drunk.

Here's another example. I could spend three hours mowing the lawn. I would mow for a while, stop and drink some beer, mow some more, drink some more beer, mow, pee, mow, pee some more. I spent more time peeing than I did mowing. Now it only takes me an hour to mow the lawn. And instead of grudgingly doing this task I consciously remind myself that I am mowing MY lawn in MY yard. I remind myself that there are millions of people who wish they had a lawn to mow. It is a mundane chore, but I actually get pleasure doing it now. I don't get pleasure from the actual activity itself – I get pleasure by redirecting my thoughts about what I am doing, where I am doing it and why it is my responsibility.

Even pleasurable or exciting activities can seem boring when you first sober up – I experienced this. When I first sober up, I felt like I should be out doing something "fun," but I had no idea what the fun was that I was supposed to be having. I didn't even know it when I was having fun. Everything in my life had always revolved around drinking, so I had no idea what fun was supposed to feel like as a sober person. During my first year of sobriety I was sad, lonely and depressed and I was depressing to be around. I realized that if I am no fun to be around, then I shouldn't be anywhere. I spent most of my time alone. In hindsight, that was what I needed at the time. It was very boring, but it gave me the opportunity to clear my body of alcohol, clear my mind of alcohol and learn what it physically feels like to be clean.

During this time I reflected and realized that I was still doing the same activities I did as a drunk – pay bills, mow the lawn, go to baseball games, concerts, movies, sex. But now as I do these things sober, I am more fully engaged in these activities. I can remember the things that I do and the people I meet. Yes, for a long time after I sobered up these activities seemed boring (well, except sex). I have finally learned how to redirect my thinking about the *perceived* boring and mundane activities. I can truly find pleasure in responsibilities. Please don't misinterpret me. I don't prance around in leotards, giddy and happy about everything I do.

Here is when boredom really hits me now. When I sit listening to drunk people talk and interact. (Time really drags when you're around drunk people and you're not drinking with them.) On a Friday or Saturday night when I'm sitting at home and I think that I should be out having "fun" – I still need to learn to get better control of this meritless desire. When my work day is over and all my domestic chores are basically done and I'm sitting all alone or on weekends when I have no plans or responsibilities.

I would be lying to you if I said that sobriety won't be boring at times. But I have come to understand that boredom is just another emotion in life. Drinking simply alleviated the boredom – at the time. But then came the aftermath and negative consequences for using drinking to alleviate boredom; falling behind in my responsibilities, procrastinating, participating in useless, dangerous or stupid activities.

My advice is that you accept boredom for what it is – a state of mind or emotion. Don't feel the need to alleviate boredom with risky or unhealthy behavior. Don't allow your imagination to overtake your thoughts – making you believe that you are supposed to be doing something "fun." This can leave you with the untrue impression that your life is mundane and unfulfilled. Don't talk yourself into expecting that every minute of your life will be filled with excitement. You can still experience joy and calm while being (or feeling) bored. Try to find joy in the mundane by being fully engaged and paying attention to whatever it is that you are doing. Remember that boredom is an emotion and every emotion does not need to be acted upon or reacted to. There are worse emotions than boredom; anxiety, fear, resentment, hatred, guilt. Boredom is real and it is inevitable.

Your Secret Support Group: People can help you without them even knowing it. I used friends and family as my secret support group. I would call them – and still do – just to talk. I ask them about what's going on in their lives', with their kids, jobs, pets, whatever. It is nice to talk about anything and everything else except drinking, sobriety, recovery – yuk. This distracts me from my own problems and temptations. These people have no idea that they are talking me through a rough spot.

I couldn't expect my friends and family to listen to me whine and cry about my struggle with sobriety forever – that gets old and depressing. There is an appropriate time and place to talk about these struggles. Keep in mind that a person who has never been through this may not know what to say or how to give feedback. Don't expect "normies" to understand or give viable advice. Nothing against them, but they just don't know.

People really appreciate me talking about normal topics with them. By doing this it reminds me that I need to have genuine interest in other people and that my conversations don't always have to be about ME and my problems. This strategy helps me get through rough spots by requiring me to focus my attention on others. It requires me to participate in normal life conversations, which also helps me feel normal.

Why can't I just drink like everyone else?: Oh boo hoo, poor me, everyone else can drink and have fun but I can't. Who says I can't drink? I suppose I COULD drink. Hell, I have every legal right to drink. So my question isn't, "Why can't I drink like everyone else?" A more appropriate question would be "Why **should** I drink like everyone else?" Here's the answer: Because I'm a drunk – plain and fucking simple – and I can't control my drinking once I start. If I try to control my drinking, I can't enjoy my drinking and if I want to enjoy my drinking, I can't control it. It sucks, but that's just the way it is. If I were to ever start drinking again I'll be the only one responsible for running my life right down the toilet.

I know that if I allow myself to have one drink today, I'll talk myself into having two drinks tomorrow, three the next day, then I'd probably revert back to my old habits – so I can't risk it. I won't deny that I wish I could drink. I like the smell and taste of beer. It smells inviting and I want to guzzle gallons of it. I like the aroma of Scotch. I like the way Scotch would hit me as I was drinking it. I like the flavor and the hard impact that straight Gin gave me. I like the taste of liquor and the sensation of getting drunk. If I deny these feelings then I am not being honest with myself. Honesty and truth allows me to respect what alcohol does to me. It sucks – I want to drink – but I honestly know I shouldn't, so I don't.

Questioning why I can't be a social drinker may be the hardest part about staying sober. There is a lot of temptation to have a couple of drinks. Every day I can come up with a list of reasons why I should have a drink, and a lot of them sound like pretty good reasons. Shit happens in life and I start to rationalize, "I deserve to have a drink." Even outsiders and friends will agree that a person should be allowed to have a drink or two when tragedy and adversity hits. (For me, the "big ones" seem to be easier to live through than the small problems.) When major emotional events occur – deaths, divorces, breakups, firings, etc. – some people might say you deserve a drink, or that falling off the wagon would be justified. *There is never a justifiable reason to drink*.

Successes and achievements can be tempting situations as well. (I have more difficulty controlling temptation when things are going well.) Drinking to celebrate an achievement is socially acceptable. You get a promotion – have a drink. Buy a new house – have a drink. It's your birthday – have a drink. Someone gets married – have a drink. Holidays especially suck and can be a challenge. Every commercial says, "Your holidays won't be merry unless you drink XYZ." I start to think, "I can have a drink, just this one time." It's so easy to think that *maybe* I could have just one drink, or limit myself to a couple.

Thoughts about trying to be a social drinker are always lurking in my mind. If I crack and have one drink, then I'll have to start my sobriety all over again and that would suck even more than sobriety. I simply have to accept the fact that I can't be a social drinker. You may be asking yourself, "I wonder if I can go back to being a social drinker?" Probably not. If you never were a social drinker or you're a binge drinker, it's too difficult to control when to stop. It may work for a while, but eventually your inebriated thinking will take over and you'll start having "just one more." For those of us that have always overdone our drinking, once alcohol is in our bloodstream it clouds our rational thinking. We're addicts, and no matter what our addiction is, we can't do things like normal people. We drunks seem to always have to do everything in excess. Once we start, we usually can't stop.

I have been posed the argument, "An overweight person can eat in moderation. Why can't I drink in moderation?" We all need to eat food, drink water, breathe and poop to stay alive. But even too much of those things can be harmful to our physical and emotional health. We don't NEED alcohol to stay alive. Moderation isn't fun for an addict. Ask any person with an overeating disorder if they like dieting or eating in moderation. They would say, "Fuck no. I would rather be chowing down six Quizno's and a carton of ice-cream right now." Why torture yourself? Why gamble against the odds? Total abstinence from alcohol is your best answer.

You may also be thinking, "Can I just drink one day a month?" Why? To get completely shit-faced and make a total ass out of yourself once a month? All you'll be doing is mentally torturing yourself. Your entire life and thinking will revolve around waiting for that "one day a month." And if you can talk yourself into drinking one day a month, you'll talk yourself into two days a month, then three, then four, etc. You will conjure up and devise all kinds of reasons why you deserve to drink today. Ask any cigarette smoker, coke-head or crack addict. Once addicted to something – always addicted. The first drink, first snort, first drag off a cigarette and you'll be right back to needing your junk.

Or think about this – what if *the one day a month that you drink* happens to be the day YOU get hit by a car? That's right... you're sitting at a stoplight, obeying the law, minding your own business and somebody hits you. You're fucked because you have alcohol in your blood. One day a month, a year, whatever, is not worth the risk of relapsing back into a problem drinking situation. Total abstinence is going to be your safest decision.

The only reason we drink is because we want to drink and we allow ourselves to do so. Like I said, I want to drink every day; I just make the choice that I won't.

Keep your mouth shut and act naturally: Just to let you know, a lot of people will act and treat you differently when they find out that you *used* to be a drinker. They will make references about drinking or joke about drinking, then become self-conscious when they remember that you're a *"recovering alcoholic"* and then apologize for their insensitivity. I noticed that when I have told people who are drinking that I don't drink any more they get uncomfortable and say things like, "I could quit anytime I want to," or, "I'm not an alcoholic, I never drink before work." Well guess what – I don't give a fuck – I don't want to talk about that.

In social settings where alcohol is being served, don't be the one who opens the door by announcing, "I am a recovering alcoholic." You would be treated more normally if you said, "I'm a recovering rapist, but I'm getting better." (At least people wouldn't ask you about it.) And don't comment about other's drinking. Who are you to judge? Keep in mind that no amount of lecturing on the evils of alcohol or criticizing how much someone else drinks will help make you a better person or keep you from drinking. Just because you think that getting sober helped your life doesn't mean it will be good for anybody else. An important element of your new sober life is that you *don't preach the good news* unless you are asked about it. I know it's exciting to have found a *new religion*, but don't bore people with it. You might as well walk into a stag party and say, "Hi everybody, who wants to talk about Jesus?"

142

People will more than likely end up knowing that you're an ex-drinker anyway. Whether you like it or not, people like to talk and gossip. Don't be surprised or offended if someone asks you how your recovery is going. Some people may avoid you because they aren't sure what to say to you. Some might stare – because they think former alcoholics are freaks. Who cares what other people think – you can't control their thoughts – you can only control your own. I am guilty myself of being uncertain of how to approach a newly recovered drunk. A good friend of mine informed me that his wife had gone through alcohol treatment. When I saw her at a graduation party I didn't know what to say at first. Should I ask her about it? Should I offer my input? I opted to quit worrying about her and pay attention to my own thoughts and actions.

It is easy to find yourself going to the anti-alcohol extreme. You certainly don't want people avoiding you or not inviting you to social events, parties, bar mitzvahs or poetry readings. (Well I guess it would be okay if they didn't invite me to poetry readings.) Parties, bars, weddings and picnics are no place to discuss your newfound lifestyle. If someone asks you how you sobered up or wants to talk about it, tell them to buy my book. Okay, seriously, talk casually with them or say something like, "I don't know if this is the best time or place to talk about this. We can get together for lunch or I can call you later and we can talk a bit more freely then." Use your judgment. Be smart. If it's an AA function, a religious function or a specified non-alcohol function, then the subject is probably welcome.

As a former professional drunk I can speak in depth about drinking, when to drink and how to drink too much. I can intelligently discuss beers, the various liquors and wines – what type of food they go with. I make jokes and references to drinking as if I am still a drinker. My friends have a tendency to completely forget that I no longer drink. New people that I meet have no idea that I don't drink alcohol. It puts us both at ease and allows them to act naturally.

Properly use your "Edit" button. All too often in my life and during my marriage I had failed to properly use the EDIT function in my brain's software. I would say something sarcastic or cynical, vehemently voice my opinions, felt I needed to express my feelings or shared too many private details – simply put, I talked too damn much.

I have learned that all thoughts and feelings do not need to be openly stated or expressed. Just because I have a thought doesn't mean it HAS to be said out loud. Some things (experiences, opinions, comments) are better left unsaid. Sometimes too much information or disclosure won't do anybody any good. An old saying goes; "A burden shared is a burden lightened." This could also be stated as; "I just downloaded all my crap on you – I feel great now."

Recovering and recovered drunks should keep this in mind. It is not necessary to share all the details of your past. You don't need to talk about all the crazy things you have done, all the things you ruined, all the wreckage of your past or all the mistakes you have made. You don't need to talk about your turning point, all the failed attempts or all the struggles of sobriety (I'm doing it here because that's what this book is about). Nor do you have to feel obligated to answer questions about your past. You can simply answer with, "I would rather not talk about that right now," or "why do you want to know?" This isn't some slick, smooth, evasive answer – it is proper use of your edit function.

Disclosing too many details of your past may not help the conversation or the relationship. You may come off sounding bitter, angry, pathetic or worse yet, sounding like you're a basket case waiting to relapse. I am not suggesting that you lie or be deceptive. Allow the other person to discover who you are NOW. All past experiences do not necessarily make us who we are today – they are just past experiences.

I will caution you that by not discussing your past you run the risk of being accused that you are not being open or not sharing enough. However, there is (and will be) a proper time and place for you to talk about your past, your goals and your opinions. There are also select and appropriate people to do this with. Everyone doesn't need to know everything. Spare your friends, family and coworkers all the sordid details of your drinking past. Remember that your brain's software does come with an "edit" function. Once again I will remind you – don't cry your tale of woe to your friends. Go out and have some fun and make sure that you are fun to be around.

Sobriety is not a punishment: It may feel like I am being punished, especially when I see others drinking socially, having fun, catching a light buzz. Even when adversity hits others and they say, "I'm getting drunk when this is over," I can experience feeling like I am being punished because I can't drink. Then I think, "How do people that can't eat peanuts feel? Are they being punished? What about the guy that can't eat strawberries, the lady that can't have shellfish, the kid that can't have sugar? Did their Higher Power stamp the numbers of the beast on their forehead and cast a punishment upon them too?" No – someone with a deadly peanut allergy isn't being punished for anything they did. We drunks are in the same boat, we are not being punished, we just can't have alcohol. It might help to tell yourself that you have a life threatening allergy to alcohol. You want sympathy from people? Tell anyone that offers you a drink that you have a life threatening allergy to alcohol. That will gain you sympathy. No one will question you about having an allergy, but just tell someone you're an alcoholic and they think you're a problem person filled with flaws and weaknesses. Next time someone offers you a drink try the allergy line, "I'm sorry, I can't drink, I'm allergic to alcohol. It causes me to break out in stupidity." You'll be surprised at how well it works.

Alcohol alternatives: I like the physical and social act of drinking so I have had to come up with non-alcoholic alternatives.

145

When I am offered a drink my typical response is, "I'll have a seltzer with lemon," and I leave it at that. If I am pressed with more pressure to have a cocktail I will respond with, "I can't, I have a long way to drive tonight," or, "I'm the designated driver." Whatever you do, don't go into detail or try to explain that you no longer drink, it's tough, but it's good to practice not being the center of attention.

Personal experience: One woman that I dated had no idea that I didn't drink – it took over a month before she found out. When we would go to bars or nightclubs I always ordered our drinks, so she didn't know what I was ordering for myself. One particular evening, I excused myself to go to the restroom and she ordered our drinks while I was away. The bartender made her drink and gave her a seltzer with a twist of lemon for me – he told her that I don't drink. When I returned she asked me, "All this time that we have been dating you haven't had a drink? Why didn't you tell me?" I just said, "See, you don't have to get me all liquored up to have sex with me."

Here are some ideas for non-alcoholic drinks that *look* like drinks:

- Seltzer with a twist of lemon in a short glass – looks like a gin and tonic or vodka.
- Coke with a lime in a short glass – looks like a rum and coke.
- Cranberry juice in a short glass – looks like duhhhhh.
- Non-alcoholic beer in a glass – looks like a regular beer.
- If I go to a ballgame or event where beer is sold in plastic bottles, I will ask my friend or date for their empty. Rinse it out and fill it with water.

(Dean Martin drank apple juice while onstage with the Rat Pack.)

In social settings it is better to *look* like you're having a drink. That way most other drinkers won't question you or keep offering to get you a drink. You can then answer with, "No thanks, I already have one."

Some people involved in recovery will say that you shouldn't look like you're drinking. I disagree. I found that it keeps people from prying too much as to why I don't have a drink. And some alcohol addiction specialists say that you shouldn't drink N-A beer because it will get you started drinking beer again. Bullshit! I like the taste of beer – I just can't drink it – so on occasion I will have a N-A beer. I have **never** had a relapse and drinking N-A doesn't make me want to drink a real beer. But if having a N-A beer is too dangerous for you then don't drink it.

Social drinking: Many people are fully capable of being responsible social drinkers and I have quite a few friends who do so without any adverse effects. I can't drink socially and maybe you can't either, but it's okay for other people to drink. Just because something isn't good for me doesn't mean I should tell others how to live their life. I believe that if you keep this type of attitude in mind, staying sober will be easier. I may have had plenty of problems due to my excessive alcohol use, but that doesn't mean others shouldn't be allowed to enjoy drinking. It also doesn't mean that others shouldn't be allowed to drink themselves into oblivion and shatter their own lives if they want to.

Let other people drink socially if they want to. Don't be the dick-head that has to tell everyone, "You should control your drinking." It is not your responsibility to save the world – your responsibility is to save yourself. Go out and live life with everyone else. Go about living a healthy, loving, successful and sober life – do that and you will be an example to others.

Never deny another drunk your help: There are some people in my life that I don't like and I could care less if they have miserable lives. In fact, I don't mind watching them struggle

147

through life because of the vermin that they are, but I would never deny them my help if they wanted to sober up. I may not like the person – but I will help them learn to live sober. I may limit how much of my own time or emotions I put into their recovery. It would be based on how much of their own time and emotion they are willing to put in. How serious are they about sobriety. How willing are they to accept responsibility for their actions and ownership of their behaviors.

I will never deny any other drunk my help. I feel this way because of how I was treated when I first decided to live sober. The one person that I trusted the most and that I needed the most turned on me. I was so close to suicide many times; I had never felt such intense physical, mental and emotional pain like that. I begged for that person to help me, but she didn't give a shit about me. I can't tell you how lonely that feels, how helpless I felt, how depressed, how useless life seemed. The roiling stomach, the sweat, the anxiety, the self doubt, the pain, the tears, the anger, the hate, the confusion, the serious contemplation of suicide. The desire and wanting for death to just take me from this mental agony.

Please, never deny another drunk your help. You don't have to be loving, compassionate or forgiving. Just be willing to share with them what worked for you. Let them know that when it comes to sobriety, you'll be available to talk with them. You can't do it for them. They have to stay sober on their own. Remind them of that and let them know that you will stay sober with them.

Spouse/Partner that drinks: The renewed relationship with your spouse or partner is predicated on the presumption that they are supportive of you and they are not drinking either. If they drink and have an attitude of, "Look, alcohol is your problem. Why should I quit just because you can't handle it?" Then this is not a healthy position for you to be in and sadly, the relationship probably won't work. Keep in mind that I said *probably*. You can be with a partner that drinks socially, as long as it doesn't bother or tempt you. They still need to show some respect of your efforts and not drink to excess.

If you demand that your spouse/partner stops drinking because you did, you are setting the stage for arguments and confrontation and they may harbor some ill emotions towards you. They may use this demand against you (unconsciously) as a bargaining tool. You might hear statements like, "I quit drinking for you and you still haven't changed... you don't spend more time with the kids... you don't take me out more... you haven't found a decent job... etc." The list could go on. You might even find yourself saying these things to your spouse after you have quit. Using statements like this and arguing will not help control your temptations to drink. Drinking again will not be a way of getting back at your partner, it will only harm you. Your spouse/partner needs to be *willing* to stop drinking with you and because they *want* to support you.

I want to stop drinking but my spouse/partner doesn't want to. Naturally, it's best if you both work on this together and help support each other. Your partner might not feel that they have a problem or simply doesn't want to stop. If you are married or in a committed relationship, it isn't unreasonable to ask your partner to abstain with you. If they cooperate, but do it grudgingly, this may cause more friction. If your partner willingly stops drinking with you, you then have an obligation to show them your gratitude. You need to thank them and learn to show them your appreciation for their help. This doesn't give them a license to abuse, mistreat or take advantage of you. Ultimately you have to focus on your own sobriety. With that said, it may be in your best interest to get out of the relationship if your spouse doesn't want to stop drinking. I would never want to be instrumental in advising someone to needlessly end a marriage or partnership. But the fact of the matter is that as YOU start to live sober and your partner continues to drink, you will be going in separate directions.

Can I stay sober if my spouse/partner is a social drinker? Maybe, but your chances of maintaining sobriety will be better if they don't. Your partner may legitimately be a social drinker, showing no adverse drunken behaviors whatsoever, but this environment won't be helpful during the early stages of your sobriety. If your partner has a couple of beers or glasses of wine every night with dinner, this isn't going to make things easier for you. Your partner might unwittingly say, "Mmmm, this is really good wine. Want to try a sip?" Or "This is a good Manhattan. Too bad you can't try it." Ask them to abstain from drinking for the first 90 days. If they genuinely are a social drinker, then this shouldn't be an issue for them.

Don't criticize, berate or insult your partner for being a social drinker. Why begrudge them from having a couple of beers at a baseball game or an *occasional* glass of wine with dinner? Remember: Just because you don't drink doesn't mean that other people shouldn't be allowed to drink. You ultimately must be your own judge and determine if you are able to be in this environment without falling to temptation. I personally find it easier to be with someone who doesn't drink, or at least doesn't drink very often.

Patience: When it comes to starting your new sober lifestyle, patience eventually pays off. Sometimes life *is* fair and justice is served, but it can only be experienced if you have patience. As long as you don't wake up dead tomorrow, life will go on and the universe will continue to expand faster than Kirstie Alley's ass.

I am sober for more than 4 years now and slowly but surely my life and the conditions around me have been improving. Can you believe that I would say that? Me? Mr. Cynical, Mr. Sarcastic, Mr. Living Sober Sucks. Oh sure, some things still suck (like the desire and temptation to drink), but conditions are getting better in my life because I have taken control of it and because I am sober. Problems still exist in my life, but they are different and more manageable problems now – almost enjoyable problems. I still battle with life's daily irritations, letdowns, struggles and disappointments, but life is starting to taste sweet again. It has been necessary for me to stop and take inventory of all the good changes and improvements that are developing. Sometimes we get so busy with life and sobering up that we miss all the changes that are subtly occurring. We are so busy *doing* that we forget that we *got* to where we were going.

I'm not bullshitting myself or you. It's not necessarily the conditions that have changed, it's my thinking, my thought system and my patience and acceptance that has made the conditions better. I can enjoy the conditions that exist due to my clear thinking, which is a result of sobriety. I am no longer chasing conditions to make me happy. My thinking draws happy conditions towards me and into my life. Sobriety has enabled me to think clearer. I see the world, people, relationships, conditions and my life from a very realistic vantage point. I can enjoy the "ups" as well as enjoying the "downs". Yes, I have learned to enjoy the downs and have gained a lot of strength and love from those downs.

Here's another thing I do to help me solidify my determination to stay sober. I step back and look at the lives of other people who continue to drink or do drugs. Their lives' are filled with unnecessary chaos. They may be very good people at their core, but they do dumb things and draw chaos into their life. They make bad decisions, they waste money, they waste precious moments of their life sitting in bars, they get drunk and argue with their spouses, children, friends, neighbors. I don't want any of that shit as a part of my life. I want to have my health, my job, my house. I want to have great friendships and a loving spouse and I want these people to know that I care about them too. I want to treat people with love, respect and kindness. These things are easier to do now that I am sober.

Even as I say that I am glad to be sober, this is a very difficult existence. I was once a drunk and I enjoyed getting drunk. I also did a lot of recreational drugs. Those are things that I still crave. I understand what it's like to be an addict. I was addicted to many things: alcohol, cocaine, tobacco. I may have taken control and stopped doing these things, but I am still addicted to them. I want them, I crave them, I would like to continue using them. I liked getting drunk, I just didn't like the results and consequences that came with all of my drunken behavior and drunken lifestyle. Someone who has never been a drunk or drug addict simply can't understand the desire a recovered/recovering person has for these things. They can't understand and relate to the depression that hits us when we can no longer partake in our old friend alcohol or drugs. When you can't have booze and everyone else seems to be having fun drinking and getting drunk, it can be pretty damn depressing.

In summary: My goal with this chapter has been to give you some ideas and strategies for *after* you have stopped drinking. I have had to learn how to live sober, which is not living in some made-up, fairy tale world. Life still goes on, good things still happen, bad things still happen and other people still drink. Alcohol will always be a part of the world and we have to live in this world. Just because you no longer drink alcohol doesn't mean you have to hide from society or that you are not a normal person. You will still suffer anguish, pain, temptation, doubt. Do not hide from life, draw yourself to life and you will draw others to you. Savor sobriety by living your life to its fullest. Enjoy your children, family, relatives, friends, coworkers. As a sober person, you can give and get pleasure by becoming a better lover, father, mother, husband, wife, friend, leader. Every day life will keep showing up and you will have to face it sober, that's just how it is. But you still deserve to live a fun, fully engaged, normal life – sober.

#13) Mark's Reward System.

Make this pay off.

I may not be formally trained in psychology, but I can tell you what I have learned from all my years of experience running my own business, being in sales and being involved in entertainment. *People only care about themselves and they do things that they feel will be rewarding to themselves.* This is not a criticism of humanity, nor do I want to be perceived as having a low opinion of people. This is simply an honest observation of human nature and self preservation. And you know what? Caring about yourself is not a bad thing. You *should* reward yourself and do things that are beneficial for you.

You may argue that you act out of the good of your belief system or for the betterment of humanity, your family, children, spouse, etc. You might donate money anonymously or volunteer to work with charities. That's wonderful – but you are still doing it for your own benefit. That benefit may be a feeling of goodwill within you or knowing that your family is secure. I donate my time helping with recovering drunks and counseling other divorced men. I learn a lot about myself by doing so and I benefit through the reward of knowing that I am helping other people. I foster rescue dogs because it ultimately helps me feel good.

That is why I say we are – *for the most part* – motivated to do things based on the rewards that we will receive for performing various actions and making given decisions. We drink or do drugs

153

because we want to be rewarded by euphoric and pleasurable feelings. It may be a feeling of happiness, power, strength, sex appeal, self-confidence, or maybe we want to be accepted by our peers, be viewed as being cool. Whatever we are searching for, we do things to be rewarded by whatever it is that we are attempting to achieve.

When we are a drunkard, we become slaves to the payoffs and rewards that we receive. It could be the drunken buzz, the feeling of Beer Power, an uninhibited approach towards life and social events. We go after that *feeling* of relaxation and reassurance that drinking gives us. Sometimes we feel guilty, and deep within our own soul we don't like our drinking habit, but we drink anyway. We end up wondering, "Why do I keep doing this to myself, why don't I quit drinking?" We're not stupid people – it's the automatic reward system in our mind that keeps taking over – that's when we make foolish choices.

Getting drunk is instant gratification – living sober is delayed gratification. When you get drunk, you are rewarding yourself immediately, or you wouldn't keep these destructive patterns as part of your life. The reward you get could be an escape from work, responsibilities or from your own personal problems. There is also a reward that your body, brain and mind unconsciously receive – because they are dependent on alcohol – they require alcohol to feel normal. Once you have become a slave to these rewards, it's hard to break free of them.

We *act* to gain a reward (pleasure, fulfilled desires, happiness, profit, etc.) and *react* out of fear (physical and emotional pain avoidance, loss of something, confrontation, etc.). Your brain is a very delicate and complex organ, and when it is physically polluted with alcohol it doesn't function all that well. I can go into greater detail about the various parts of our brain that drive our emotions – *actions* and *reactions* – such as the cortex (frontal lobe, parietal lobe, temporal lobe) limbic system (amygdale, hypothalamus, etc.), but that knowledge isn't necessary here. What is necessary is to understand that this organ is running all on its own without us even realizing it. Your brain wants you to reward yourself with pleasure – this takes place *unconsciously* and *subconsciously* – and as an alcoholic, you *consciously* act on these impulses by drinking, in hopes of gaining that reward.

Now that I am sober, I am fully aware and accept the fact that my brain unconsciously and subconsciously drives my thoughts, which then influence my conscious actions (whether those actions are smart or not). Understanding that *your* brain does this on its own can help you get control over your conscious reward system. This is why it is important to replace the unconscious *destructive rewards* of drinking with conscious *constructive rewards*.

It is important that you clearly define *realistic* rewards that you desire to obtain and *how* you are going to reward yourself for not drinking. Just so you know, I stopped drinking with the hopes that I would be *rewarded* with a happier life and a revitalized marriage. How did that work out for me? My marriage collapsed, I feel like a failure, I lost more than half my stuff in the divorce and I struggle with regaining my self-confidence. However I must be getting some sort of reward out of sobriety otherwise I would have gone back to drinking by now. I am not always able to see the immediate daily rewards of sobriety – I am counting on future rewards. I want a happier relationship with a loving spouse, better health, financial stability, higher personal productivity, improved self image and a better life in general.

If you are going to consciously make the decision to eliminate alcohol from your life, then it is important that you plan on having some replacement rewards. Enjoying replacement rewards will bolster your willpower and confirm for you that living sober is worth the effort. Take look at your own reward system a bit closer. What can you do to give yourself some of those feelings of immediate gratification for staying sober? Here are a few examples of rewards for you to consider.

Positively based rewards: Think of all the money you won't be wasting on alcohol. Think about all of the wonderful things you will be able to afford (a new HDTV?). Think about the wonderful vacations, movies, shows, and recreation you will be able to afford for your family. Think about the hobbies and activities that you will be able to afford and be better at. Think about how you will become a more productive, high-paid and valued employee.

Positively based rewards don't have to be exclusively materialistic. Think about the loving relationships you can rebuild. The friendships that will grow deeper. The clarity of your own thoughts. The personal pride and higher self-esteem you will feel. How much healthier you will be. Think about the great sex you will be able to have while sober.

Negatively based rewards: Indignation and anger can be powerful motivators. Think about all of the people that you will show that they are wrong about you and that you DO have self-control. Think about all the foolish behavior that you will no longer have to apologize for. Think about all of the drama that you will eliminate from your life. Think about all the other people that will be getting arrested for drunk driving. Think about all the shit that they will have to deal with in their lives'. Think about all the losers and doofusses that you will leave behind.

It *IS* all about the money: Americans are going through some very tough financial times: Layoffs, debt, cratering home values, foreclosures, losses in retirement funds. (But during boon or bust, it seems like drunks always have these problems.) It's times like this when getting drunk seems like a good way to escape. But I can assure you that you cannot drink your way out of financial problems. Doing so will only make things worse. Maybe the loss of a job and tough financial times can be your catalyst to start living sober? Maybe it will at least cause you to cut back a little? After spending some time getting your financial malaise under control, you won't go back to your old habits as readily. Once you have enjoyed the power of self-control and have experienced the financial rewards of living sober you won't want to lose that feeling when your financial situation turns upward again.

I got sick and tired of always being broke, wondering were all my money went. So within the first 30 days of sobering up I started a mutual fund that I deposit money into every month. This is money that I would have been spending on booze or drugs. I could always find money to spend on beer or Scotch, so now I do the same for my mutual fund. It may not be a lot, but it adds up pretty quickly. I plan on spending that money on either another car or a vacation some day. I also spend my *booze money* on good food. I buy steak when I want; I treat myself or a friend out to dinner. I'm not using money to make myself happy; I'm rewarding myself for NOT drinking it away.

So how much money have *you* wasted on drinking? This can be a painful but eye-opening exercise. Do some of the math on the "Drunkards Worksheet" located at the end of this chapter. Once you have a rough idea of how much you waste on alcohol and all the peripheral shit that goes along with it, think about what you would do or like to do with that money, if you had it now. It's a rude awakening to see the numbers on paper. But don't torment yourself for past wrongs. You can't go back and change what has happened, you can only make today better and plan to be smarter tomorrow.

Start a Savings Account: I suggest that you start a separate *Sobriety Savings Account*. This should be a *Passbook Savings Account*. The reason I want you to start a Passbook account is because you physically have to take the Passbook to the bank to withdraw money. You can't simply access or withdraw money online. Physically having to go to the bank will give you time to think whether you really need to take this money out or not and you won't be so easily tempted to impulsively spend it. As I've mentioned, you could always come up with money for drinking, so for every day that you don't drink, put $10.00 into this savings account. You know that you spent at least $10.00 a day on drinking. So instead of stopping at the bar every day on your way home from work, stop at the bank and deposit $10.00 into a savings account. Yes – do it every day! The bank doesn't care how much or how often you deposit money, that's what they're there for. The reason that I suggest you make a deposit every day is twofold: First, you want to make it a habit, and second, if you let that money pile up on your dresser that fifty bucks looks real tempting at the end of the week – you might end up spending it on something foolish. Do this for one month and you'll have $300.00. Stay sober for 90 days and you'll have accumulated $900.00 and after one year you will have saved up over $3,600.00.

Think about it. After only 90 days of sobriety and saving your booze money, you'll have $900.00. What could you do with that money? A new HD-TV? A fun vacation? New clothes? New furniture? Reduce debt? Gifts for your spouse or kids? This simple strategy alone is worth the price of this book.

If it's not a savings account, then you might consider a mutual fund. Send $50, $100, or $200 a month to a fund (or set up an automatic monthly draw from your sobriety savings account). You decide what you will do or want to do with that money after only one year. Stash away half the money you would normally spend on booze or drugs and use the other half to pay off bills or give yourself small rewards occasionally. Having more money available can calm you and make you feel more secure and give you a sense of self-control.

Drunk, depressed and broke is not a good combination. Don't drink for 30 days and start a savings account. What's the worst that can happen – you can end up with more money at the end of the month.

It isn't just money that helps me enjoy my sober life: Now that I am sober, I find that I use my mind and my time far more efficiently. I enjoy my work and my projects more. I reward myself by spending more time playing with my dogs. I spend more time working in my yard and making my house look nice. I spend more time helping friends with their home projects and I spend more time having deeper relationships with my friends. I go to a gym to exercise, which rewards me with better health and higher levels of self-esteem. I read a lot of books to further my knowledge. I stay very busy doing things for me, my family and my friends. And when I'm just sitting around *fuckin' off*, I don't feel guilty – I can truly relax.

I'm not suggesting that you have to become a super-human overachiever to enjoy life sober. Just the fact that you won't have to deal with drunken drama, chaos and lunacy may be reward enough for you.

Mark your calendar: I have a calendar on my fridge that has green circles around each date that has passed. I use a green magic marker to make these circles, which represents every day that I have lived sober. I also write in monthly anniversaries. My friends know what the green circles mean, and if a newcomer asks, I can proudly tell them what the circles stand for. I also place a green $ symbol in each day that I put money into my booze savings account. This is a silly little exercise, but it works well as a visual reminder for me. I am over four years sober and I still circle each day.

Devise your own reward system so that you can see, feel and enjoy sobriety. Little rewards will make sobriety seem worth the effort in the short term. The long term rewards of sobriety will take care of themselves. So how will you reward yourself?

Drunkards Worksheet

Here's a simple little worksheet for you to write on. Use this sheet to figure out how much money you currently spend on alcohol and other alcohol related expenditures.

How much do you spend on liquor?

Do you drink at home? _____
Alone or just when entertaining friends? _____
How many nights a week do you drink?_____
How many drinks per night? (be honest) _____ / $_____
Do you buy alcohol for friends or spouse?_____ / $_____

Do you go out drinking? _____
How many nights per week or just weekends? _____
How much do you spend (average) when you go out? _____
Do you buy for other people when you go out? _____
Do you smoke when you go out? _____
Add cost of cigars or cigarettes._____
Breakfast after drinking, food and snacks at bar? _____

Cost per day = $_____ X # of days per week

= $_____ per week.

X 52 = $_____ per year.

How many years have you been drinking? _____

Based on just these questions, how much do you honestly think you have spent in a lifetime? _____

Alcohol related expenditures:

O.W.I. tickets? _____

Increased Insurance cost? _____

Legal costs? _____

Jail time? _____

Stuff you have broken while drunk? _____

Stuff or money that you have lost while drunk?_____

Stuff or money that you have given away while drunk _____

Things you bought while drunk; drugs, lottery tickets, etc? _____

Stuff that you have bought, that you didn't need, while drunk? ___

How much do you think you have spent in total?
$_____

What else would you or could you do with that money?

_____

_____

_____

_____

_____

#14) Sobriety and Creativity.

A tortured soul can spark creativity – but don't go out of your way to torture yourself.

From a wounded soul can flow a wellspring of creativity. It's almost like you have to visit hell before you can write a travel brochure about the place. Quite a bit of comedy, song lyrics and art come from the mind of a tormented past. Notice that I used the word *past*? Creativity is a way of releasing and sharing these past troubled experiences in a constructive form. These experiences then bring joy and beauty to others while relieving pain from the soul of the creator of the art.

Some people are under the belief that they only way they can tap into their creativity is through the aid of mind altering substances. While chemically altering the mind with alcohol or drugs may generate some interesting, bizarre and even valuable ideas – are these creations the expression of the true person or just the result of substance influence? While this may work at first and you might experience a few successes along the way, the substance overtakes the mind and flattens the creative process. Or worse yet, the substance allows the mind to have a delusional impression that what it is generating is creative and good – when in actuality the ideas are shallow and useless. Using a mind altering assistant to aid in creativity becomes a crutch. The creator (you) then believes that the only way *in* is through your substance of choice.

A simple illustration would be a person who thinks that they can dance better after a few drinks. They feel uninhibited, express themselves openly on the dance floor and experience more popularity. Ah, but after a few more drinks they don't dance as well, in fact they may even make a complete fool out of themselves. They can't see their own actions but still believe that this 'crutch' is what enabled their creative dancing expression to flow. They come to believe that they have to repeat the process every time they go out dancing to be comfortable and popular. Then the substance takes control over them and their true creative flow is flattened. How many people have you witnessed make a complete ass out of themselves on the dance floor at a wedding or think they're really good at karaoke after *one too many*? You may contend that a couple of drinks helps to loosen you up a bit when you go out dancing. I agree, this might help overcome inhibitions, but for some of us (like me or you) who have no control over alcohol once it is introduced into the bloodstream, this is a dangerous and loosing gamble.

Sober creativity: As you slowly become comfortable with sobriety, your creativity will resurface and you might discover a whole new creative side to yourself. Exploring and releasing your creativity will comfort your troubled mind, reward your desire to be useful and reinforce your determination to live sober. Creativity satiates the appetite of wanting to be constructive and productive.

What if you never were a creative type person? Was that only because you were always drunk, lazy or both? If you have spent most of your drinking career hanging out in bars, sitting around watching TV or just being lazy, then you need to find where your creative seeds are and nurture them. It doesn't matter if you are clumsy, an uncoordinated oaf or creatively mindless, there is something creative that you can do. This is where I must revisit having fun, playfulness and visualization again. Each of these requires you to use your imagination.

Seeing yourself hitting a walk-off homerun in the World Series is fictitious dreaming (unless you're a MLB player). However, fictitious dreaming is playful and fun. It is not to be discounted, because when used properly, it leads to the creation of realistic and attainable goals. You can start by seeing yourself in the World Series, and then begin working your way backwards – visually – from the walk-off homerun. See yourself as a position player for your favorite team, see yourself at team practice, see yourself working out in the gym, and see yourself as a talented ball player. With these visualizations you can now see yourself hitting the game winning homerun for your local softball team – a realistic and attainable goal. I know that this is a silly example, but I use it as a parallel so you can use your own imagination to create your own personalized fictitious dreams. Dream big, then work backwards – visually – to see yourself reaching attainable goals.

Imagining future events requires lucid thinking. This is what sobriety allows for. Now that you are sober you should try new things. Use your imagination to visualize yourself doing something creative. Is it playing a sport, playing in a band, painting, singing, decorating your house, building something, being part of a group or movement? Consciously think about these things as you lay in bed before falling asleep (unless of course you're having sex, then please pay attention to that). Spend time in a quiet environment to daydream and allow your imagination to flow.

The *types of* and *desires for* creative release are different among everyone and creative capabilities vary even more. While natural abilities play a big role in what is a pleasurably rewarding creative release for an individual, not having a natural ability at something is no reason to avoid creativity. For instance, I love music but I don't have the natural knack for playing an instrument. Others can pick up any instrument and start playing it right away – they could virtually play the French Horn with their ass – which is how I always thought it was played – hence my never being allowed to join the school band. My lack of natural musical talent doesn't mean I shouldn't pursue my desire to learn how to play an instrument. I would be learning and playing for my own pleasure.

You may have been wrongly told by someone in your past that you are not creative. We are all naturally good at something and every human wants to be creative, even if it's simply for our own personal pleasure. Do not limit your pursuit of creativity because someone else told you, "You don't have talent," or "You aren't creative." But be realistic in your expectations of the results from your creativity. I am realistic in knowing that I would never be able to make a living as a studio musician, but I can still enjoy the creative release of playing, practicing and annoying my neighbors with my off-key music.

As I mentioned earlier, a large amount of creativity comes from, and is rooted in pain. Song lyrics, music, comedy, painting, writing, artwork – many of these are forms of creativity that reflect a suffering soul. If you are feeling pain, release it through these outlets. Creative works of this type don't have to be for public consumption. There's nothing wrong with creating something just for your own entertainment and enjoyment. It's the pleasure that you get from looking at your own work or doing something yourself that makes it worth your time and effort. Dig into your deepest emotions and let your feelings guide your creative channels.

Just start working on projects and hobbies or try a new hobby that you've always been interested in. Bear in mind that you may not be very good at new things when you first sober up. Your hands and mind may not be as stable as you would like them to be. Just keep working at being creative. Creativity and hobbies will divert your mind away from thinking about drinking. As you become healthier and more stable, you will become better and more proficient at your activities. This will spark feelings of worth and accomplishment. It is at that point when you need to push even harder at your creative talents. You might surprise yourself at how good you are at something.

Creativity doesn't always have to be expressed through a physical product – you can donate your time and be creative. Volunteering is a great creative outlet (and you can make mistakes at someone else's expense). Activities you might consider include helping out with functions at your local school or church. Helping to teach the illiterate to read. Campaigning for a local politician. Working at a local V.F.W. Post, Salvation Army or reading to old geezers at a nursing home. You don't have to become the next Mother Theresa, but simply being part of a cause that you feel is worthy *is creativity*.

Personal experience: All during my drinking years I was highly creative. I had a modestly successful career in radio comedy and was quite entertaining even while I was a drunk. (I'm sure I'm biased in my opinion of myself but my radio and entertainment achievements can support my statement.) I wrote and produced some of my best comedy while drinking or drunk and most of my performing was done while intoxicated. I wasn't always completely hammered while doing creative projects, but alcohol *seemed* like it was a creative lubricant. I would do remote broadcasts or go out and make public appearances for radio stations while I was drunk. I wasn't an angry or argumentative drunk when out in public (my ex-wife may not agree with this statement) and I was only called on the carpet once by management for being drunk at an appearance. I didn't need alcohol to build my courage or make me funnier – drinking and getting drunk were just a natural part of my life.

I worried that I wouldn't be funny or creative after I quit drinking. Hey guess what? I was right. I would sit in my living room and stare out the window like a neutered cat. It would have been nice if I could have licked myself like a neutered cat – that would have broken up the boredom a bit. My concern that I would lose my sense of humor and creativity was one of the key reasons I didn't want to quit drinking – at least that's what I kept telling myself. I thought that the only way I could be funny and creative was if I was drunk – that's because I was usually half drunk all the

167

time. In any case, my lack of creativity and humor lasted for only a short period of time when I first sobered up.

When I began my sobriety all my conversations with family and friends became very philosophical and delved into heavy topics (quantum molecular physics, electro-spectroscopy, why is snow cold... that sort of thing). At first, all I could talk about or wanted to talk about was being sober and staying sober. It's tough not to talk about your problems or talk about staying sober when that's all your mind is filled with – that was the focus of my being at the time. Holding normal conversations about everyday subjects could be a chore. It seemed like the topic of sobriety, alcoholism or my marital woes would always surface. I could be talking about deep sea fishing and the next thing I know I'm talking about how bad of a drunk I was, how mean my wife is or how her friends are undermining my sobriety and reconciliation efforts. I had to pay very close attention to where conversations were going and their subject matter.

Don't get me wrong – I still had my sense of humor. I would still make funny comments, satirical observations, wise cracks or jokes about being a drunk and what we drunks do. Most important – I still laughed. Not as much as I used to, at the same things or as heartily – but I laughed. Even though I was slowly gaining my sense of humor back I could still be a depressing person to be around. My wife even nicknamed me "The Depressor."

After about four months of sobriety I began being funny again. As I passed nine months of sobriety, my friends started commenting on how interesting, fun and engaging I was becoming again – instead of being "The Depressor." Friends now say that they really enjoy the *sober Mark* much better than the old *drunk Mark*. Now when I make new acquaintances they are drawn towards me even quicker (this could be due to my Rasputin stare or my really smelly pheromones). I don't tell people that I'm a recovered alcoholic, so these new friends have no idea what I was like as a drunk. As a sober person I am far sharper and wittier. I am much more conversational, animated and engaging (and modest). I am able to write more vibrantly and quickly express my thoughts. This has opened up new avenues of communication for me such as writing witty blog entries, humorous website articles, emailing pictures of my butt to friends or sending silly text messages.

Being sober will steady your hands and mind, which will then allow you to work on more mentally and dexterously challenging projects. (Now that my hands are steady I have taken up the hobby of shaving hamsters.) I was always good at construction and I built a lot of impressive stuff when I was totally gassed. But now that I am sober I can sit down, visualize mechanical projects, draw them out and build them even better than I ever did as a drunk. I make fewer mathematical and mechanical errors (plus I'm far safer with power tools). I would always drink beer while doing home repairs, mechanical projects or creative work. I still do those same repairs, projects and creative work – I just do it sober. I am much faster at it and I have a much more positive and aggressive approach towards these things now. I feel a higher level of confidence knowing that I will be sober and smarter as I undertake new projects and challenges. I go out of my way to try new challenges. Because I can accomplish things faster, I get more things done. This allows me to enjoy my recreational and relaxation time much more. The adage "success spawns success" does hold true.

In summary: My creativity was not completely lost when I sobered up. It became subdued for a while, but it has come back in a different and more powerful style. I have learned that the creativity is here, waiting inside of me and I don't need alcohol to unleash it. I have also learned that everything I create doesn't have to be a masterpiece. Some creative efforts are done for personal enjoyment. Others are never used or never come to full fruition but they spark the next creative task. Now I challenge myself to be more creative. I know that I have the crisp mind to undertake projects I had never tried before. If I fail, so what, I can try again or hopefully I am smart enough to try something else. The act of creativity, and creative thinking, makes sobriety bearable.

Use this time to discover new talents you have living within you. Sitting around idle and brooding will only make sobriety seem more like a punishment – which it isn't. New hobbies and creative activities will help you expand your circle of friends and acquaintances. This may be a lifesaver for you, especially if you had to purge your social circle of drunken acquaintances. You may find new strengths that allow you to be more socially outgoing, productive at work or involved with your family. You might discover a skill that you are very good at which turns out to be highly profitable for you.

#15) It's easy to forget the pain.

The paradox of time.

A s I get further away from being a drunk, I forget how crazy my life was as a drunk. I have forgotten what it feels like to wake up with a hangover, to not remember what I did, who I argued with, who I might have pissed off, what stupid thing I might have said or done. I also seem to have forgotten about all the pain I endured while sobering up. The months of physical, mental and emotional hell. It's easy to forget all of that.

As my sobriety passes with time, my determination to stay sober strengthens, but the powerful temptation to drink again strengthens as well. This is a paradox which causes a battle to ensue within my mind and with my emotions. Consciously, I can tell that I am much healthier. I feel better about myself emotionally, physically and personally. I know that in many ways I am a better person now. I know that I have deeper and better friendships now. I spend far less money, I work harder and smarter. But I don't always feel any happier – I still suffer from doubts about whether I even needed to sober up (I will elaborate more on this shortly). This is when it gets tough to maintain sobriety.

It wasn't just the social part of drinking that I liked, I enjoyed drinking alone too. I liked getting drunk, I liked the act of drinking and I liked the flavor of whatever I was drinking. I wish I could have physically drank more without getting as drunk as I did (sometimes it wasn't fun getting that drunk). That's the shitty part about drinking too much – forgetting things, breaking things, losing things, saying stupid things. The things that you can't get back, have back or statements that you can't take back. All this comes with the drunkenness and I tend to forget that part. *The memory of being drunk is better than what it was actually like being drunk.* It's so easy to forget the bad times, because I can't remember them – it seems better than it was.

I have heard from fellow drunks and substance abuse therapists that certain time lines and anniversary dates make this get a bit easier. At 90 days you feel a big empowerment, at six months you feel more comfortable with the new you, at one year you notice that your thinking has cleared and you're feeling *normal*. This is not becoming easier for me. The level of temptation changes, the triggers change, and it seems to get harder as I get more accustomed to living sober. Some things are easier, such as having a better understanding of why I can't have "just one little drink." Saying "no" is easier, but I'm not necessarily having any more fun in my life. I must be even more vigilant now because life is filled with temptations to drink.

For example, I had some guests over to my house on a warm, sunny, Sunday afternoon. I had never met these people before; they were friends of a friend. They are a very nice couple, have two normal young children. We headed out for a casual boat ride. All of the adults grabbed a beer out of the cooler – I grabbed a can of Non Alcohol beer. The guy next to me says, "What, you're not having a beer? You trying to clean up or something?" He meant no harm or insult, it was a natural question. Instead of me making a big deal out of it or explaining that "I'm a recovering alcoholic," I just said I have to drive the boat and directed the conversation towards something else.

I didn't care that other people were drinking in front of me, but truth be stated, I wasn't having much fun – I wanted to drink too. I couldn't get mad at them because they can drink. I couldn't bring their mood down by lecturing them about temperance. I couldn't simply go hide in the house while everyone else goes out and has fun. (I felt a level of sadness because I wished that my wife would have been there with us, reminding me how proud she was, helping me to forget about my temptation. She wasn't there and I had to deal with this on my own.) It sucks that I have to be afflicted with this addiction and I have to struggle with temptation 24 hours a day.

Here is another example of how easy it is to forget the pain. My best friend Mike got engaged and picked a date to marry his new girlfriend. Mike asked me to be best man at his wedding and I was highly honored by his request. One of my duties as best man was to organize a bachelor party for him. So I invited a group of guys over to my house. It was your typical setting... cigars, beer, foul jokes, inflatable doll, etc. We hung out at my house for a couple of hours. All the other guys were drinking beer but I drank seltzer and O'Doul's (N-A beer). These guys know that I don't drink and none of them tried to tempt me or bust my balls for not drinking. The subject of me not drinking came up and we talked about it briefly. Most complimented me on my ability to stay sober – but it was a party for Mike – so we stayed focused on teasing him.

We eventually left my house and headed out for dinner at Hooter's – I was Mike's designated driver. While we were eating dinner, the subject of "not drinking" came up again. The other guys were all drinking beer and I was drinking iced tea. As we talked about drinking, some of the guys that have known me for many years began to say that I wasn't a bad drunk. They commented on how I never got belligerent and "You never got sloppy drunk... why can't you have a couple of beers? What's the big deal?"

Was it just *their perspective* that I never got sloppy drunk or belligerent – they're drinking. How do they know what might happen if I were to drink? They wouldn't have to deal with my

173

guilt or the aftermath. I could see how it's much easier to talk someone *into* drinking than it is to talk them *out* of drinking. These are the dicey moments when friends can unintentionally influence you to drink again.

As I thought about what they were saying I began to question myself whether I *could* drink. I wasn't seriously considering drinking then and there, but I started to wonder about it. Suddenly I began to feel anxiety rushing through me. I became warm, my heart beat faster, I started sweating, I began feeling terrified. I thought, "What if I did have just one beer and they were all wrong? What if I couldn't stop at just one? What if I did get all drunk, sloppy and belligerent?" What was I thinking? How could I even think this way? My mind was running a million thoughts at once – but no one could sense what I was going through. Outside I was calm, but inside I was raging with panic. This was all too scary for me.

I slowed my mind down and I posed this question to myself, "Would drinking improve my life?" The answer was a simple "NO." None of my friends would have thought any less of me if I would have had a drink, but I would have thought less of myself. I didn't have a drink – not because I am so strong or because I didn't want to break my sobriety streak. I didn't have a drink because I answered the simple question, "Would drinking improve my life?"

I am baffled by how I could have forgotten about the problems excessive drinking brought me, the pain and torture I suffered while sobering up. I am even more stunned by how quickly the thought of drinking entered my mind. I know how much anxiety and terror I felt just thinking about drinking and I can only imagine how much anxiety and terror I would have felt if I would have had a drink. After one drink I would have felt even worse and the only answer would have been to have another drink, and another and another. I am so glad that I followed my own advice and slowed my thinking down during those few important seconds when I could still say "no." I saved my own life. I'm sure I will have to do it again. If I am ever tempted to drink I will ask myself the very simple question, "Would drinking improve my life?" The answer will always be the same... "NO."

Did I really have to sober up? This is an example of how doubt and temptation was able to gain a stronger foothold during the first year of my recovery. I spent a fair amount of mental energy asking myself the question "Did I really need to sober up?" My main reason for quitting drinking was to salvage my troubled marriage – but that ended anyway. At first glance it seemed to me like sobriety had been a wasted effort. So I needed to ask myself a different question, "Had I continued drinking would I still be married?" I don't believe so. My wife and I both drank – our consumption and disconnection would have progressed. Her actions outside of our marriage were her own decision. Had I continued drinking I likely would have acted more inappropriately myself, made costlier decisions, did more dangerous things, bringing on greater levels of chaos and drama into my life. Who knows what bigger problems would have come to pass.

As I moved further into sobriety, I felt as if my life was becoming more dysfunctional. I wasn't enjoying my work, I felt peculiar in social settings and I didn't look forward to seeing the next day. While bills were being paid and I was reducing debt, I couldn't sense much positive progress in my emotions. After my divorce I was filled with greater doubt about my decision to live sober. Upon honestly accepting the reality of what I did during my marriage – and what my wife had done – I lost all feelings of self-worth and self-confidence.

It has only been through sobriety and the passing of time that I can see how my failed marriage had nothing to do with my decision to live sober. My lack of self-esteem and self-confidence has nothing to do with sobriety. Loneliness, despondence and *perceived* failure have nothing to do with my sobriety. All of these negative feelings have to do with my own actions and my own thinking.

175

After about one year of sobriety I was finally able to answer my question of, "Did I really have to sober up?" The answer was simplistically clear – *Yes! My chances of achieving happiness, loving relationships and material success are far better sober than if I were trying to do this drunk.* I am able to comprehend the power of this answer. Consciously reminding myself of this statement along with always asking, "Would drinking improve my life?" allows me to have control over my temptations to drink.

Living sober may suck, but life is meant to be enjoyed. But how can that be? How can such complete opposite statements go hand in hand? Pleasures in life come with things that "suck". Here's an example. I own six dogs and it sucks when I have to pick up dog shit, but dog shit happens to come with dogs. If I want to enjoy the friendship, fun and love I experience with owning dogs, I must also perform a duty that sucks. The same applies for cat owners, horse owners, cleaning the aquarium, working for a living and living a sober life.

Living sober may suck but you can also enjoy life at the same time. You owe it to your friends, family, spouse, lover, partner and especially yourself to enjoy your life. If you are religious and believe in God, then you especially owe it to your creator to enjoy your life. Life can be enjoyed after recovery and even while you are recovering from an addictive past.

I recently watched a great man die. It took him almost 3 full months to wither away, slowly degrading and spending his last month unable to walk or talk, barely able to hold his head up and focus on me. We had rare moments of eye contact. He labored with breathing, unable to eat. No feeding tube, just a slow, ugly, foul death. Right before he began fading away, he said something to me that I must try to live up to myself. He looked at me and said, "Mark, I have no regrets. I did everything I wanted to do in life."

He did not say this with arrogance or because he lived highly at someone else's expense. He said it with gratitude and appreciation.

176

He had been a farmer, a biker, a hard laborer, he worked fulltime from age 13 to age 63. This man traveled the world, skied all over the world, traveled around America on a motorcycle, hunted, fished, golfed, bowled, gambled, and dated plenty of women. He did all of that and he WASN'T a drinker. He fully enjoyed his life without drinking.

This man taught me how to ski, to hunt, to fish, to play cards. He taught me how to accept the fact that some things in life suck, like paying bills, working for a living, shoveling snow, paying taxes, picking up dog shit. But he also taught me how to enjoy all those things that suck. This man was not only a good friend of mine, he was my uncle. I will never forget the things he taught me. I want to be able to say, "I have no regrets. I did everything I wanted to do in life and I did it sober."

I sure hope this gets better: I have learned that living sober is an evolutionary process – and evolution does not always produce perfect outcomes. While I have seen the lives' of many people dramatically turn around for the better once they have sobered up, I have also witnessed others struggle, only to have relationships end, friendships deteriorate and families be torn apart. Everything doesn't always work out for the best, but you can make the best of how things work out.

Many areas of my life have improved as a result of sobriety (physical health, mental clarity, friendships, financial prudence, self-discipline). Some have gotten worse (feelings of loneliness, self-doubt and regret). I am counting on things improving, but only by staying sober. I know that the only way I can continue to develop personally – which will result in better relationships, rewarding work and materialistic gains – is by staying sober, consciously paying attention to my moods, feelings and actions.

On October 12, 2009, I passed four years of sobriety. I talk very little with friends about my struggles with alcohol and the difficulty of getting over my ex-wife. These subjects rarely come up in conversation any more. If they do, I am able to joke about being divorced, my past drinking exploits and my sobriety. I act so normal now that friends forget that I don't drink. That should be a good thing, but it's a reminder to me that *now* is when I must stay ever vigilant.

Daily problems, temptations, triggers to drink, friends and social environments are constantly changing. Making the decision to quit drinking altogether was a huge step – living the rest of my life sober is going to be an even harder task. I sure hope this gets better.

#16) I'm lucky to have been an alcoholic.

I might be in a hole but at least I've stopped digging.

Alcoholic – what a wonderful title to hold. For us problem drinkers, being an *alcoholic* is a badge of honor. It gives us a sense of being part of an elite group or club. Other drunks welcome us in with open arms. Then, if we stop drinking, our new title allows us membership into another exclusive group – the *recovering alcoholics*. We're special; not everyone can be a member of either of these groups – I am a member of both.

While I was actively drinking, I wasn't embarrassed to admit to other drunks that I was an *alcoholic*, I would state it loud and proud. And I wasn't ashamed of my drinking escapades – hell, I joked about it – my friends joked about their drinking too. Not only was I an alcoholic, I was a *good drunk*. When I say that I was a *good drunk* I mean that I was gracious – I always had a wide variety of beer, wine and liquor for my friends and guests. Wherever I went I always brought plenty of beer and liquor with me to share. I freely bought my fellow bar patrons drinks. I never owed anybody money for booze and never had a running bar tab. I also know my liquors quite well – which wine goes with what food, which liquors mixes well with what, and what kind of buzz you can expect from certain alcohols. As any *good drunk* should be, I was well educated in my hobby.

179

But now since I quit drinking, I have had to deal with the stigma of, "He's a recovering alcoholic." People seem to treat me gingerly when that term is used about me – like I'm an oddball or extra sensitive. Even when I go on dates and I say that I don't drink, I am then asked, "Are you a recovering alcoholic?" No, I'm just someone who doesn't drink. Or worse yet, if I am in a relationship, meddling friends of my girlfriend will warn her, "Be careful, he's a recovering alcoholic, he could relapse at any time." I know this from my own experience. All I can respond with is, "How do they know? They're not dating me. Tell 'em to mind their own fuckin' business. If you're worried, then don't date me, or better yet, don't drink around me."

The stigma of being termed an *alcoholic* or a *recovering alcoholic* keeps many people from being willing to share their struggles. They are worried about the embarrassment that their friends, family or partner will have to endure. But guess what? Chances are good that your friends, family or partner is already aware that drinking is causing problems in your life. And which is worse? The stigma of being a recovering alcoholic or letting alcohol run your life?

It is my belief that the title "Alcoholic" is overused as well as misused. Someone does not have to be clinically deemed an alcoholic to have problems in their life due to drinking. Some people want to belong to this exclusive group – *alcoholic* – to gain sympathy or attention. They like holding this title so others will show them compassion and forgive their behavior. Calling one's self an alcoholic also allows people the opportunity to offer an excuse for their behaviors such as, "Oh I know I'm such a fuck-up, but I can't help it... I'm an alcoholic." Or, "I can't quit drinking. I've tried but I'm an alcoholic." We often use the title "Alcoholic" so we don't have to accept responsibility for ourselves and our own decisions.

It's nice to be able to blame something else for our mistakes, indiscretions and failures. "I'm normally not like that, it was the

180

alcohol," or "I was drunk, I didn't know what I was doing" and "I can't help it, I'm an alcoholic" are great excuses. And the nice part about using alcohol as an excuse is that alcohol can't defend itself.

The harsh reality is that "I'm an alcoholic" is not a valid excuse. You don't have to be a stereotypical *raging alcoholic* for drinking to adversely affect your life. Maybe whenever you have a couple of beers you get lazy and don't feel like fulfilling your responsibilities. After a couple of glasses of wine you have a tendency to argue with your partner. Anything that gets in the way of you performing your daily responsibilities or creates conditions in your life – that you don't like – is a problem.

Say for example that I loved *Crafting* and I spent all my free time crafting. I am so busy crafting that I don't eat properly, don't mow my lawn, bathe, perform my duties at work or show up to non-crafting events. People would simply say that I am obsessed with crafting but they wouldn't give me the title "Craftaholic" or suggest that I go through a 12-step program to stop crafting – but it is still a problem for me.

The difference between alcohol and crafting (golf, fishing, tennis, Sudoku, etc.) is that once alcohol is self-introduced into the body it physically changes how your brain interprets signals and stimuli. If you have the "terrible habit" of crafting too much, you can always set time limits; "I will only craft for two hours tonight," and you can stop crafting after two hours without it affecting your thinking process. Whereas if you said; "I will only drink for two hours tonight..." you wouldn't be able to think as clearly afterwards, providing that you could even stop drinking after two hours.

If you thought that crafting, Sudoku or fishing was getting in the way of your daily functions, you know that the best way to control that problem would be to not even participate – you would abstain. When it comes to something as powerful as alcohol – and if drinking is causing problems in your life – the best way to control the problem is to abstain. I am fully aware that the only way I can guarantee I will never have a problem with alcohol is to totally abstain from drinking it. It's the FIRST glass that is the problem – not the last.

Quick education on how alcohol does its magic: Alcohol acts on the nerve cells within the brain. Alcohol interferes with communication between nerve cells and all other cells, suppressing the activities of excitatory nerve pathways and increasing the activities of inhibitory nerve pathways. (This means your brain gets numb but you feel like taking your pants off). Alcohol affects various centers in the brain, but these centers are not equally affected by the same BAC (Blood Alcohol Content). Some areas of the brain are more sensitive than others. As the BAC increases, more and more centers of the brain are affected.

The order in which alcohol affects the various brain centers is as follows:

- **Cerebral cortex**
- **Limbic system**
- **Cerebellum**
- **Hypothalamus and pituitary gland**
- **Medulla** (brain stem)

The cerebellum coordinates the movement of muscles. The brain impulses that begin muscle movement originate in the motor centers of the cerebral cortex and travel through the medulla and spinal cord to the muscles. As alcohol affects the cerebellum, muscle movements become uncoordinated. (This is why you slur your speech, bang into shit and fall over.)

Your brain and your actions respond to alcohol in progressive stages, which correspond with the increase in your BAC (Blood Alcohol Content):

- **Euphoria** (BAC = 0.03 to 0.12 percent)
  - You become more self-confident or daring.
  - Your attention span shortens.
  - Judgment is not as good – you may say the first thought that comes to mind, instead of something appropriate for the given situation.
  - You have trouble with fine movements, such as writing or signing your name.
- **Drunk** (BAC = 0.09 to 0.25 percent)
  - You become sleepy.
  - You have trouble understanding or remembering things (even recent events).
  - You do not react to situations as quickly (driving, being punched in the face, etc.).
  - Your body movements are uncoordinated.
  - You lose your balance easily.
  - Your vision becomes blurry.
- **Confusion** (BAC = 0.18 to 0.30 percent)
  - Might not know where you are / what you're doing.
  - You get dizzy and stagger.
  - You get highly emotional – aggressive, withdrawn, crying or overly affectionate.
  - You cannot see clearly.
  - You have slurred speech.
  - You may not feel pain as readily (like when you get punched in the face).
- **Stupor** (BAC = 0.25 to 0.4 percent)
  - You can barely move at all, let alone stand or walk.
  - You may begin projectile vomiting.
  - You lapse in and out of consciousness.
- **Coma** (BAC = 0.35 to 0.50 percent)
  - You are unconscious.
  - You have a lower-than-normal body temperature.
- **Death** (BAC more than 0.50 percent) - You usually stop breathing.

It gets better. Alcohol has two noticeable effects on the hypothalamus and pituitary gland, which influence sexual behavior. Alcohol depresses the nerve centers in the hypothalamus that control **sexual arousal and performance**. As BAC increases, sexual behavior increases, **but sexual performance declines**. In layman's terms: You think you want to have sex but you aren't very good at it. Men get whiskey-dick and a woman gets a dry koochie – you can't perform and then you pass out. Cool huh?

This data is not an anti-alcohol diatribe – I am simply relaying some physiological information on what alcohol does to the human body. I would hope that by now you know that I am not some temperance lunatic. Alcohol is fine for those that want to drink it. Many people are responsible social drinkers and alcohol doesn't pose a problem for them in their life. Some people are complete drunks – great – good for them, if that's what they want.

Back to why I'm lucky to be an alcoholic: I was pretty damn funny and very quick-witted when I was drunk (at least I think I was). Too bad I can't remember many of my best jokes. I do remember most of the things I did when I was drunk, but on occasion, I would get drunk enough where I was not able to remember things. I could be highly engaging and entertaining when drunk, (again, I think I was) but I'm sure that I annoyed the shit out of plenty of people (I'm sober and I still do). As I have frequently mentioned, I was a functional alcoholic. I accomplished a lot of things while I was half in the bag. It's too bad that at the time I didn't realize how much of a problem my drinking was causing for me and my relationships. Only a few people miss the *Drunken Mark* (namely the owner of my local liquor store, some bar owners and Budweiser stock holders).

So why would I feel lucky to be an alcoholic? For one thing, I don't think I ever would have clearly seen that I needed to make such dramatic, conscious changes in my life. This meant that I not only had to address my drinking problem, but also the way I look at and approach life. I had to honestly analyze and reflect on my actions, my relationships and my thinking process. I wouldn't have had the chance to put myself through the humbling experience of looking at my own flaws, faults and defects – the areas of my life that I do have control over and that I can improve. I may have never come to fully accept the fact that I am totally responsible for my own actions, my thoughts and how I treat people. I never would have gotten to know my real friends and family as deeply as I have.

Being broken down and humbled is similar to going through boot camp. You get reduced down to a total "nothing" and you build yourself back up from there. You use self-discipline and self-control. The stronger you get, the better you get at it, and the prouder you feel. It might be beneficial for everyone to go through a self reflective improvement program a few times during the course of their lives. I certainly plan on doing this for the rest of my life.

Having been an alcoholic and an addict has enabled me to be understanding to what other addicts struggle with. It has allowed me to appreciate the suffering we go through while we're actively drinking and while we are trying to heal. I have tasted the sweetness of success and felt the bitter pain of failure – all while I was both drunk and sober. The pain and the struggle is what make life so vibrant. Without the pain I wouldn't be able to fully appreciate the pleasures.

Having been a drunk makes me a bit cynical towards advertisers and the media. Advertising and social pressures make drinking look and seem glamorous. That's okay. I take it for what it is. I laugh at all the beer commercials that show hip, cool, good looking people drinking and dancing or the dorky looking guy picking up beautiful women. They never show a drunk guy puking in the bushes, relieving himself behind his car or waking up next to some hideous beast that he doesn't know. But then, I wouldn't expect to see that in a commercial, they're trying to sell a legal product.

Drink a little and enjoy it. Drink a lot and pay the consequences. Having been a drunk myself helps me see through all the hyperbole, the rationalization and denial we drunks live with. It's pretty hard for a drunk to bullshit me.

Having battled with alcohol, tobacco and cocaine, I now hold a higher respect of what addictions are and how they can control our lives. I have come to the belief that all addictions are not destructive. A desire, like, passion or even an obsession for something doesn't make it bad and destructive – as long as you can control it. I have also learned that virtually anything can become a destructive addiction. Most people would view alcohol, recreational drugs, smoking and gambling as bad addictions. These items may not be healthy for you, but they aren't necessarily bad addictions if you can control them and they are not problematic for you. Golf, bass fishing, NASCAR, Stamp collecting – can become a destructive addiction. A destructive addiction is something that not only affects you; it negatively affects the lives' of people around you. I am now able to objectively analyze my hobbies and activities, see if I am being too obsessed with them, see if they are getting in the way of my daily functions and harming others, then take corrective action if necessary.

Being a recovered alcoholic has also allowed me to see the world in very honest terms. I am not shocked or let down by others' transgressions. I may be a bit cynical at times, but I realize that we are all fallible and most people are simply trying to do the best they can. I try not to let the world and events that are out of my control bother me. I allow nature to take its course and I don't take bad luck personally. Life is usually better than what I think it is, but less than what I want it to be. I can also see through bullshit better. Con-artists, liars and cheats are no longer held as "hopeful deals" in my eyes. I see them for what they are and I quickly move away from associating with them.

I have learned to be much more open-minded and realize that my way is not the only way. This enables me to see other peoples' perspectives much clearer. I am open to understanding others' traditions, religions, political beliefs, preferences and culture. This doesn't mean that I simply fold and agree with them, I am just more willing to hear their point of view. This has opened up many new friendships for me and allows me to remain calm when I don't agree with something. This also causes me to think, "Maybe they are right, what can I learn from them?"

Going through the recovery process and rebuilding myself has opened me up to letting small accomplishments feel highly rewarding. I have learned how to enjoy simple pleasures in life. My mind and senses are so much more receptive and aware. But this is a rusty, double-edged sword, because along with the mental clarity comes the painful acceptance of personal responsibility. I can all too vividly remember the mistakes I had made in my life and in my marriage. I am haunted by my own past actions. I begin to ruminate over all the bad things I did, wishing I could go back and change them. Then I struggle with guilt, frustration, anger and the temptation to drink those memories away. Then I see my dogs playing and wrestling, start laughing, and forget about all the bad shit... for a while... I know that it'll be back.

I feel that my sense of humor is sharper, quicker and more searing. Now when I insult you, it's not the booze talking – I sincerely mean every cutting remark and insult I make – my putdowns are much more personalized. (When I think about it, I may have been an even bigger asshole all my life had I not been drunk.)

I am far from being the perfect person, in fact, I'm not even close. I do feel as if I am making progress at being a better friend and I hope to be an even better husband again one day. I feel calmer and more enlightened. I will honestly admit that I had some of the best times of my life completely drunk. I have done a lot of wild, fun and exciting things that no sober person would ever do. But I also have to admit that I probably wouldn't have fucked up as many things as I did in my life if I wouldn't have been an alcoholic. I wouldn't have wasted so much of my time and money if I wouldn't have been an alcoholic. I may not completely like where I am, but it's better than where I was, and I wouldn't be here today if I would never have been an alcoholic. Ya... I might be in a hole, but at least I've stopped digging. I guess that's why I say I'm lucky to have *been* an alcoholic.

#17) Hints for the alcoholic and nonalcoholic.

Try talking.

I'm sure I could have continued my life in the same drunken way for years. I would have wasted more money, broken more things, failed at more career attempts and my health would have deteriorated. I'm certain that my wife and I would have continued to grow further and further apart, eventually getting divorced anyway. I would have also missed out on getting to know my dad, my sister, my brother and my friends as well as I have.

Only through sobriety can I clearly see that I had a serious problem. But at that time I was drunk, delusional and unaware of all the failures unfolding right in front of me, all by my own doing. I reflect and wish that I would have asked for help. Had I done that, I might still be married right now. I *feel* completely responsible for ruining my marriage. My wife was the best thing that ever happened to me in my life and I lost her. I was an obnoxious drunk and pushed her away. Regardless, I wish I would have sobered up sooner or asked for help sooner.

I am not making excuses, but to my recollection, no one ever sat me down and seriously talked to me about my drinking problem. I'm sure that some did – I just wasn't listening or didn't want to hear it. Maybe some people wanted to talk to me about it but they were afraid to confront me. I fully understand that it is no one else's responsibility to correct my errors or save me from myself. With that said, I still wish someone would have talked to me.

Veiled suggestions and expressions of loving concern had no effect on me. Counseling or consoling wouldn't have worked. I needed to be talked to in straight forward terms and in a language that I understood. I wish I would have been given clearly defined ultimatums. I wish my wife would have said, "My bags are packed and waiting by the door. If you don't sober up and work on our marriage with me, I am leaving you." I may have gotten defensive, I may have felt as if I was being threatened, I may have said, "Mind your own fuckin' business." But at least I would have been made aware of the gravity of the situation and it would have been my choice to either hear someone out and correct my behavior, or do nothing and live with the consequences. I am not blaming anyone else. It wasn't someone else's responsibility to intervene or straighten me out. I am the result of all my own decisions. I am paying the price *today* for what I did *yesterday*.

What I find as mildly confounding is even sober people offer excuses. After two years of sobriety, I asked my sister why she never said anything to me about my drinking. My own sister said, "What was the point of talking to you about it? You wouldn't have listened anyway." Who knows, maybe she's right? Maybe I wouldn't have listened? So not only do drunks avoid addressing their own problem, the sober people involved in their life often avoid it as well, and time just keeps on ticking by…

Addressing the alcohol problem.

In this section I want to relay some ideas on how a persons' alcohol problem can be addressed. First I will reach out to us drunkards, and then I will direct my suggestions to those of you who want to help us drunkards.

To my fellow drunks: If someone has come to you and expressed concern that they think you have a drinking or drug problem, you probably do. Friends, spouses, lovers, coworkers and family members don't go out of their way to potentially ruin a friendship or relationship with you if you haven't shown some signs that you have a problem. These people typically aren't trained in addiction psychology. They will be very emotional because they have gotten to a point of frustration, so they may not approach you in the best way or say the right things. Having someone talk to you about your drinking or drug problem may seem annoying, but you should actually feel honored that someone loves you enough and cares about you enough to put themselves in an uncomfortable spot. If you love and trust the person that's approaching you, please listen to what they have to say. Don't argue with them, let them say their piece. Maybe they see something you don't.

Asking for help: If *you* think you have a problem, you probably do. It can be difficult and embarrassing to admit to yourself and to someone else that you have a drinking problem. This is the tough part for you because once this has been stated; you are now in a position where you have to do something about it. That's why it is imperative for your success that you seek help from the right people. It doesn't have to be a trained counselor, but it should be someone who truly knows you intimately and has a desire to help you live sober – not just another active drunk who would prefer that you keep drinking with them.

When deciding on who you are going to talk to, it must be someone you trust and respect. Consider talking with your spouse, lover, parent, brother, sister, relative or best friend. If you don't have confidence in any of them or they don't exist, then consider your boss, a clergyman or an alcohol counselor.

Once you have decided, make a real appointment with that person. You have to take this seriously and show respect for their time. Ask to meet with them in a quiet setting so you will be able to talk privately and uninterrupted. (This could be at your house, their house or office, a lunch engagement, coffee shop or

191

bookstore.) Let the person know ahead of time that you are going to be opening up with them. Make certain that this okay with them.

When you meet with this person, be prompt and DON'T drink (this might happen if you go to lunch, dinner or meet at a house). You should both agree to certain terms regarding your conversation. Agree that you will both maintain confidentiality. Let the person know that they can speak freely without you getting shitty with them. It is imperative that you shut up and listen. Don't argue, don't get mad, don't interrupt to defend your past actions or habits. Be prepared to hear some things that may hurt you or that you don't agree with.

An example of how you might begin, "I believe that alcohol is getting out of control in my life. I need to get some honest feedback from you. I want to ask you some questions." Then ask the following pointed questions:

- ✓ Do you think I have a drinking problem?
- ✓ Have you ever seen me get so drunk that you were embarrassed to be around me?
- ✓ What kind of stupid things have you seen me do?
- ✓ What kind of drunk am I – Do I get rude, argumentative, silly, or am I an overall fuck up?
- ✓ Am I a jerk just when I'm drinking or am I always a jerk?
- ✓ How do you think I can improve?
- ✓ Would you be willing to help me stay sober?

These are just a few example questions – make a list of personalized questions that you would like answered. (Remember, you asked, so don't be an argumentative asshole.) Maybe you aren't as bad of a drunk as you think you are. Maybe you're just a grumpy, depressing asshole and alcohol isn't your problem. You might be surprised at how people perceive you and your actions. We don't always know what we look like through other peoples' eyes. The most important part of this will be for you to take the feedback to heart. Reflect on what the person says or suggests, be introspective and think what actions you should take. If you determine that you in fact do have a problem with alcohol, decide on a plan of action. What are you going to do about it? Will this person be willing to support you? Are you willing to undertake this plan of not drinking? When are you going to start?

For concerned friends, family and spouses: At what point should *you* talk with someone? Do you wait until they have already ruined many aspects of their life or other people's lives? What do you say? How do you approach them? When do you approach them? What gives you the right? Here is my opinion if you sincerely believe that someone you know has a drinking problem.

First of all, just because you don't drink or are a recovered alcoholic yourself isn't a reason to accuse someone else of having a problem. Or simply because someone else drinks more than you typically do doesn't mean they have an alcohol problem – don't go on a witch hunt. Don't take it upon yourself to feel as if you need to save the world or correct everyone. Second, be aware that just because you have a sincere talk with someone about their drinking doesn't mean any good will come of it. Some people will get extremely defensive if you tell them you think they have a drinking problem. Some might not want or appreciate your help – they may tell you to "go get fucked." Keep in mind that someone that has a drinking problem either doesn't think they do, or they don't want anybody lecturing them about it. Don't expect the person you are approaching to say, "Gee, thanks for pointing that out to me, I didn't know I was such a fuck up." How would you feel if someone told you they don't like the way you live your life?

Don't approach a person about their drinking while they're drunk. They're not going to listen to you or even comprehend the gravity of what you are telling them. While someone is drunk, they may agree with you just to appease you – to get you to shut up – then keep right on drinking. I have had people call me when they're half in the bag and want to talk with me about quitting drinking. I don't get shitty with them, but I try to talk about other stuff. I will say, "Hey look, I'll talk to you about anything but sobering up while you're drunk. You're obviously not serious about this or you wouldn't be drunk." You might think this is the wrong approach on my part and I should be willing to help at any moment the plea comes in. But I'm telling you from my own experience, that when someone is drunk, all of their future plans sound brilliant to them. They have all sorts of wonderful intentions – but they're still drunk – and all plans are rapidly forgotten when they open their next beer, bottle of wine or fifth of Scotch. Drunks can be sneaky fuckers – I know, I was one. My time and your time are too valuable to listen to some blubbering drunk crying about their problems. The term 'drunk dialing' ring a bell?

If you honestly feel that someone's drinking is creating a problem in their life, or between the two of you, then make the decision to say something. Be sure you have a clear vision and understanding of that person. Be very certain about your observations of their drinking. The confrontation that you are about to have may ruin your relationship with them – possibly even end it forever. Be damn sure that you are ready for anything to happen.

The same method should be taken as I suggested for those seeking help. Ask to make an appointment with the person so you can talk privately and uninterrupted. Tell them that you want to talk about a very serious matter. Agree to certain ground rules for this meeting. Let the person know that you are going to open up with them. Ask that you will be allowed to speak freely. Ask them not to drink before this meeting or during the meeting. Make sure that these ground rules are okay with them. If they don't want to agree, then there is no point in meeting.

At this meeting talk straight forward and honestly. Don't dance around the subject or try to put a happy spin on it. For example you might say something like, "Paul, you're a good friend of mine and I'm concerned about your drinking. I may be out of line or overstepping my bounds, but you are so important to me that I feel I should say something. You can tell me to get fucked and mind my own business, but I really do want to talk about this. Can I tell you why I'm concerned?" You may have to ask twice. If they don't want to talk, so be it. If they *do* want to talk – give them honest examples of their drunken actions and what problems you think are coming their way if they continue to drink. Then shut up and listen to them. Let them tell you if they feel alcohol is a problem for them.

At this stage, if they are opening up, the best way to be of help is to ask a lot of questions – don't lecture. You may have to go slow to get them to open up. Ask why they think drinking is a problem for them. Ask what reasons they think they have for drinking. Ask how they envision their life without alcohol. Ask what types of things they might want to accomplish, own, do or experience if they were sober. Ask if they want to get their drinking under control. Ask if they want your help. Don't expect the person to change after one conversation. It may entail many conversations and a lot of your time.

That is the 'Catch-22' of wanting to help someone sober up – YOU have to be willing to follow through and be committed, just as much as the person that wants to quit. It's easy for you to say something helpful or talk about recovery, then walk away. You go home to your normal, happy life and the person you're trying to help is left all alone wondering what to do next. Helping someone else is a lot of work, but you will get a lot out of it too. You have to be willing to spend time with the other person doing things that don't involve drinking. You need to be available to talk – at any hour of the day or night. You should be willing to open up your home as a sober refuge. You have to listen to your own words. You may uncover some things about yourself and learn how you can be a better person as well.

Ultimatums: I tread delicately on this subject. The last thing I want to do is be instrumental in fucking up someone's marriage or relationship. But sometimes there is no other alternative than an ultimatum. Occasionally this must be done not just for the sake of

195

the other person, but for your own health, safety and future. An ultimatum is simply stating, "If you don't quit drinking, then I will leave you." When you propose an ultimatum like this, you must be prepared to follow-up on your part of the demand. If you don't follow-up on your end, history will just repeat itself and nothing will change. Plus you won't be taken seriously in the future. Sure, one of your requirements might be met for a while, but then the drunk person will try to test the limits of every other stipulation you have laid out. Active drunks are sneaky when all they want to do is drink. You can be flexible with your requirements of the other person but you must be *inflexible* on what you are prepared to do. Be absolutely, positively, completely 100% certain that you have tried every method and have exhausted every other option before presenting an ultimatum. Once you have placed your demand out there, there may be no turning back. Not only will the other party have to deal with the consequences, so will you.

When do you use an ultimatum? When your safety is in jeopardy, your children's safety is at risk or your future is on the line. You may have to be willing to give out an ultimatum such as, "Your drinking is creating a problem between us. If you are not willing to work on this with me, I am leaving." This cannot be an idle threat. You must be prepared and ready to follow through.

The other side of an ultimatum will be the agreed upon actions you must carry out if you gain the other person's cooperation. It is even more important that you work together as a team if they are willing to agree with your request. Gaining an agreement from someone is a HUGE success. It means that they value you enough to address their problem. This does not give you a license to abuse your power. You cannot expect or demand that the other person work out their problem all on their own. You now have a responsibility to work as a team. It will require patience, compassion, flexibility and effort on your behalf. You will have to spend more time together maybe even go to counseling together. You can expect a few snags and difficulties as you work on this together. It may not work out as you hoped or planned but you

196

have clearly made progress if the other person is willing to try.

No guarantees here: I do not guarantee that ultimatums will work. I do not guarantee that talking with someone about their alcohol problem will have any positive effect. Alcohol is an inanimate enemy that completely takes command over an alcoholics' mind when it is in their system. Nothing will change until the alcoholic is willing to exert self-control and willpower to keep alcohol out of their system. The best advice I can pass along is to just keep trying. Keep offering your help, keep doing something. You have to believe that at some point a breakthrough will occur. I realize how simplistic and hokey that statement sounds, but other than totally giving up on a person and walking away, what alternative is there?

Sobering up may be the greatest thing that ever happens in someone's life. They may rekindle friendships and restore loving relationships with family, spouse and children – and you might be an instrumental part of it. I will not lie and say that these things are guaranteed to happen or that this will be fun and easy. I will say that it is worth the effort.

#18) Blah, blah, fucking blah.

Is this goof still talking?

This final chapter is a series of **Essays, Short Prose** and **Journal Entries**. These writings just didn't fit into any other chapter but it is my belief that they are important statements to ponder while learning to live sober. I have learned through my work with other alcoholics that you just never know what little nugget or statement might be the one that clicks for another drunk.

My intention is not to share my tale of woe, speak poorly of anyone or paint myself as a wonderful person. I am not looking for sympathy. My purpose here is to share the wild emotional and mental swings that will take place – and how these states will change while sobering up. These have not been edited or updated. They may include spelling and grammatical errors (oh, like the rest of my writing doesn't). Some of this is painful, some insightful, some funny but most are the ramblings of a recovering drunk. This is just how I felt at the time.

I realize that I have spent a good portion of my story boring you with the happenings and failures of my marriage. I did this to illustrate that we will all encounter obstacles that get in our way while working at living sober. In my case, the sadness of my failed marriage, the ensuing divorce, the deaths of my father and uncle all made me to want to drink but I was able to stay sober through it. I understand and accept the fact that drinking will not bring my wife, father or uncle back to me. Some things in life just plain and simple suck.

Essays, Prose and Profundities:

I have come to the belief that things do happen at the right time, but only when we can actually see them in front of us and we are ready for them to happen. This is not by the hand of some deity or through destiny – but due to my own sober consciousness. Things do happen for a reason and not always for the right reasons or for the best outcomes. I'm learning to let things happen naturally.

I'm not saying that you just sit back and wait for the world to unfold in front of you, or that you take a defeatist position and allow the world to happen to you. You do have to take the initiative and sow a few seeds, and you can't expect everything good to happen all at once. Allow nature to takes its course. I am learning that the things that we hope for may not necessarily be the best for us at the time. It is often when things didn't happen as I had hoped I am able to say, "Wow, I'm glad that didn't turn out like I was hoping it would." Life is a result of random happenings. None of these happenings are at the wrong time… they are all just at the time. That's just the way it is. Life can go into the crapper without any warning, without any reason. Enjoy what is, when it is. It all turns rotten at some time and then hopefully it gets better.

I hear people say, "Whatever happens in life will be the best for you." Well my response to that is, "Fuck You! How the fuck do you know what would be the best for me? Bad shit happens to good people and good shit happens to bad people. There is no balance or ledger system in life." Life isn't fair. It doesn't all work out in the end. It's disproportionate, and God could care less. Why should God care? She's given us a free will to act on our own.

There are a few clichés that recovering drunks commonly use, such as "Live and let live" or "Let go and let God." Well how about a couple of new ones like "Hey, if you don't like how your life is – shut the fuck up and do something about it," or how about "It's YOUR problem – not God's – so deal with it."

There are no substitutes for sobriety. Becoming a religious zealot will not do it. Intelligence won't do it. Furthering your education will not do it. Moving to a different city, finding a new job, finding some other addiction or substitute will not do it. Sobriety is all that it is – living sober. No excuses, no lies, just living sober. It's not necessarily that exciting.

Alcoholics are not all alike. We have only one thing in common, we drink too much. Other than that, we are all unique. Some drunks are mean, some violent, some become sexually uninhibited, some are funny, some love to dance when they're drunk. We all act differently when drunk and we each have different stages to our drunkenness. When we finally decide to start living sober we tend to look for other activities to take up the time we normally spent drinking. We also seem to be under the impression that life will become exponentially better. Life doesn't automatically get better for every one of us once we are sober. In many ways my life got worse. My daily problems got louder and larger and I had no way to escape reality. Many days I don't even want to wake up, but I lie to myself and say, "Today is the day that I will do something right." What else can I do? If I don't try, I die.

You are the only person that can help you. It sounds easier said than done. It's easy to talk when it's not happening to the person giving feedback or advice. But hey, I lived this bullshit, I've been through the pain, I've battled through the mental torture I imposed upon myself. I have experienced the psychological anguish, racing thoughts, thoughts of suicide, thoughts that life didn't matter. I have cried myself to sleep - when I could sleep. I have woken up crying, hating myself for everything I did as a drunk... I have been to hell.

I still have to forgive myself and learn to face the current consequences of my behaviors. Forgive yourself. Promise yourself that you WILL be a better person in the future. Get over whatever bad stuff happened. Try to make good with people you have harmed. It may not work, some people may not care that you want to make good, it honestly may be too late.

Some of us are fortunate enough to have a good streak for a while. Some people happen to be born with good looks, higher intelligence, higher learning capacity, a wealthy family or all of these conditions. They're members of the "Lucky Sperm Club." Most of us are just a result of what happens around us and have to make our own happiness. We have no control over where or what traits we were born with. The universe will gladly continue expanding without any one of us. All we really do is consume things, air, food, water and all we give in return is waste. I am not angry, cynical, spiteful – maybe a bit depressing. I've been through my fair share of crap. Some days life tastes pretty good, other days it sucks. Make the best of what is, but remember that there are consequences that will always have to be paid.

It is not right for me to whine. I am blessed with fantastic friends. However I am still curious and wonder about the nature of my friend's motivations. There must be *something* that my friends want or hope to gain from me. I'm certain that I don't make myself available as a friend for no self-serving reason. There is no such thing as unconditional friendship or love from people. Maybe at some point in a crisis it is unconditional – at that moment – but at some point in time there will be a reckoning. I clearly must want something out of a friendship or relationship. I give something, I don't know what. I want something, I don't know what. Never make any useless acquaintances. Friends play a larger role in our life than we may realize, whether helpful or harmful. Be a good friend, and maybe you will be lucky enough to have good friends in return. I have wonderful friends. I must be doing something right.

Think for a moment about all the different kinds of friends you have. They come in all shapes and sizes. Not just race, gender and physical traits, but levels of friendship. There are acquaintances; those are the friends that we have in our school or job. These are friends because of common conditions we live under. There are friends that we have that are based upon common interests, groups or an intellectual plane. Then there are friends that we connect with through our hearts. Those are the precious people that we experience the intimacy of stimulating conversation, camaraderie and love with. Try to develop friends in each of these categories. Try to have a few friends that cross all of these categories. Risk hurt, become a friend. We ain't got shit if we ain't got friends.

My advice is to not take your sadness out into the world with you. Don't take your sadness or depression to work. Don't bring your family down, don't bring your friends down. When I go out in public, I am happy. I'm vibrant and people like hanging around me. I am not hiding from my issues, I'm just trying to live a normal life. We are drunks and we have enough internal problems, don't bring any more drama into your life or the lives' of others. Just because you feel like God pooped in your coffee cup doesn't mean you should bring everyone else down around you. I may be struggling inside, but I won't bring others down. This helps me to be a better friend and to stay sober.

#1 - Don't take depression with you out into your life.
#2 - Don't cry your "tale of woe" to everyone you run into.
#3 - Do your best to always be in a good mood while you're around people.
#4 - Get a pet. Become a dog or cat owner.
#5 - Celebrate sobriety by going to dinner with friends or hosting dinner at your place.
#6 - Exercise! It really does help you feel better about yourself.

Who knows what will trigger your temptation to relapse. Being depressed and staying depressed will make you weak and you are more prone to give in to temptations. Depression tricks you into rationalizing that you "deserve a drink." You may have a hard day at work, an argument with your wife, husband, family member, somebody pissed you off. Don't let anger or depression trick you. Catch yourself and decide to do something else other than drink. Even if it's for 10 minutes. Do something to get your mind off of anger and depression. Those few seconds when you can still say "no" are the most important seconds in your continued sobriety.

For some strange reason, I am more tempted to drink when things are going good than when they are going bad. When shit starts going right, I feel like celebrating my accomplishments. That is when I have to build on my success and strength. I remind myself that I was able to accomplish a challenge only because I am sober. It can be tough to stay sober when you're having fun. I might be hanging out with friends or sitting on the neighbor's deck, or at a party. The drinks are flowing and everybody is having fun. I must remind myself that those few seconds when I can still say "no thanks" are the most important seconds in my continued sobriety. Remember to reward yourself. Enjoy your power, bask in your strength, then humble yourself and do something nice for a friend.

Journal Entries:

These entries were written during some of my hardest emotional struggles. I bounce around a lot with present tense and reflecting to past tense. I was just writing - I wasn't sure if anything would make sense. See - I told you my mind was all goofy for a while.

(*November 18, 2006*) You have to remember that I spent the last 23 years of my life with someone. I spent my life with the same woman, my partner. My every thought was always as a team. When I made my commitment to be married, that was it, that was how I thought, as a team. I never imagined any other way of thinking. Oh sure, I wondered what it would be like if I ever became a widower. I ached inside just thinking that my wife might go before I did. I never imagined going through the hardest challenge of my life so alone. I have no idea what it feels like to be

204

happy, sober and loved. I know what it feels like to be sober. I know what it feels like to be happy and I know what it feels like to be loved. I have not had the opportunity to experience all of these sensations simultaneously.

I am not saying that the only way to be sober and happy is with another person. I am just not used to being alone. I have had wonderful family and friends helping me out along the way. My adult life had always been spent with a partner. I am now sober and lonely. Being this way is not fun. It sucks the way my life is now. I would much rather be drinking. However, I am confident that if I was drinking, and I had still gotten divorced, my life would be even worse. I don't know, I think that I may have been happier had I stayed a drunk. Alcohol works as a wonderful social lubricant when you need the courage to go out and get yourself on the market. My statements might sound confusing and perplexing, hell, I'm confused and perplexed. I might think that I would prefer to be a drinker, but I have now experienced enough "up side" to sobriety that I won't go back. I can't risk experimenting to find out if I am capable of going back to being a social drinker.

(*January 6, 2007*) The absolute worst time I have ever experienced in my life was the first year after I stopped drinking. I was sad, depressed, lonely, I cried almost every day, I didn't want to wake up in the morning. I was always tormented by the desire to drink just to escape from the world, escape from my pain, escape from my loneliness. Sounds real fucking inviting doesn't it? As I sit and write this I have to tell myself that this is just part of the re-building process. This is supposed to make me stronger and allow me to get to know myself and my strengths and weaknesses better. I sure hope it works.

Don't misinterpret that I am lonely, sad and depressed just because I lost my friend alcohol. It is true that when you stop drinking for good, you are giving up an old friend that you have had for many years. Most of my pain comes from the fact that my marriage and my life fell apart. I did so many things to fuck up my marriage BEFORE and AFTER I stopped drinking. My marriage and relationship with the woman I loved actually got worse after I quit drinking. My wife continued to drink, and brother let me tell you, she DRANK! She was making up for all the booze I wasn't drinking. She and her friends would pound bottle after bottle of wine at my house, right in front of me. I would stay sober and they would make fun of me. They would say how pitiful and pathetic I was, make cutting remarks about what a freak I was and how "clingy" I was towards my wife. NO SHIT I was clingy, I needed help to get me through this! These were people that I had shared my home with, my food and my booze. I had done many a favor for these people over the years, and they just stabbed me in the back.

So as far as AA Step #9 goes (make amends) some people don't deserve my amends and they can just go fuck themselves. I don't believe that you have to apologize to everyone. I don't think there's anything wrong with hating some people. You're only human, don't try to act like a saint. I may be a sober, calmer, more compassionate, wiser and understanding person now, but some people can still go fuck themselves as far as I'm concerned. I don't brew and stew over my anger about people that have done me wrong. I can't let anger control my thoughts or purposefully go out of my way to make other people miserable, but I do think that a little anger is good for a person. I believe that you shouldn't deny yourself the opportunity to feel every emotion known to mankind. These emotions are what make life what it is - the good, the bad, the happiness, anger, loneliness.

It's irrational for me to say that I am completely lonely. I have the best friends and family in the world. I am amazed and honored by how many people truly do care about me and want to help me. These are friends and family members that would bear my pain for me if they could. They love me that much, so how can I say that I am so lonely? I owe it to these people, the people that stick by me, to have a happy and productive sober life.

I know that I have to stop allowing myself to bathe in my own self-pity. Self-pity is like being a hamster in a wheel. You just keep running on it and you go nowhere. I will admit that it's not easy to block out self pity, but if I didn't, it would just wear me down, I would start to feel even worse, and then I would feel even more self-pity and then I would feel even worse (i.e. hamster wheel). Allowing myself to wallow in self-pity would stir up feelings of anger within me. I would get angry at myself, angry at my wife, angry at my situation, angry at seeing other happy couples, even angry at the God that I wasn't sure existed. Yup, even though I didn't completely believe in "God," I still got angry at Her.

During my first four months of sober living, I was personally able to fuck up my life into a confused mess. I did almost everything that AA and other programs suggest that you don't do. I went into a new career field and got a new job, I moved out of my house, I started searching for new friends, started my divorce process, and drank N.A. Beer. I'm not sure if doing these things helped or hurt me, I just thought that they were the right things to do at the time. I didn't have the support of my wife to turn to and tried to think out all of these decisions on my own. Most of the things I did and changes I undertook helped me to stay focused on my goal of sobriety. Even though I did a lot of stupid things while I was sobering up, none of them compare to ALL the stupid shit I did as a drunk.

(*January 18, 2007*) My greatest recreational pleasure - aside from sex with my wife - was going to Las Vegas. I went there to drink and gamble. I had the luxury of going to Vegas about every three months or so, and when I got there, I drank. I would stay up for days just drinking and gambling. I don't know if I was as annoying as other drunks but I know I was an asshole with my wife. I didn't treat her as well as I should have. When I got to the blackjack tables I would tell the cocktail waitress, "Keep them Budweisers comin' 'til I fall out of this chair." Sadly I never fell out of the chair… I just kept drinking - for days. I would rotate between Bud, Scotch, Bombay Sapphire then back to Bud. First I had to have a couple of Bloody Marys. My goal was to drink more in dollar value than I lost gambling.

I am 15 months sober and finally making my first return trip to Vegas. I wonder how I am going to handle the temptation to drink? I'm four months divorced, had just left my job that I had worked non-stop for over one year, I'm single, horny and heading to Vegas. My goal is to have fun, be myself and stay sober. My other goal is to NOT cry my tale of woe to others and bore them to death. There were so many major changes taking place in my life. I don't even feel like I am alive. I feel as if I am walking around in someone else's body. This all feels surreal, almost like a sense of déjà vu. I think I am dreaming. It is weird, too weird for me to explain in words.

(*January 21, 2007*) Once I got to my favorite hotel, the Las Vegas Club, I immediately started to settle in. As soon as I sat down to gamble, it all came flooding back to me. I was surprised that I was still able to have fun and I actually enjoyed gambling while sober. I believe I did a little better gambling, because I was able to think more clearly and made wiser bets. I was feeling great about my self control. I was all by myself, I could have had a couple of beers or I could have gotten blasted out of my skull. I could have drank all I wanted to. Who would have known? I was alone and I wouldn't have to tell anybody that I'm a healing drunkard. For all I know I might have been a much more engaging and entertaining person if I would have drank. I think it would have been easier to control my urge to drink if I would have had a friend with me. I believe I would have been less tempted to drink if I was able to watch a buddy drink. I don't understand why I feel that way, I just do.

I noticed how quickly some people get drunk. Maybe my sobriety allowed me to pay closer attention and observe others' various stages of drunkenness. Some people would get a little goofy, others would get slurry and sloppy, while even others could go from "happy drunk" to "asshole" to "total fuck head" in under an hour. It made me wonder which one of those I personified? I'm sure that I was each one of them at some time or another. I found it interesting that the dealers, pit bosses and cocktail waitresses noticed that I didn't drink. Most casual gamblers in Vegas drink, so I stood out to the staff. I'm just saying that they noticed this and were very pleasant and talkative with me, more so than they had been in the past when I was a drinker. The other gamblers that I would talk with at the tables didn't notice that I wasn't drinking because I look and act like a drinker. I have a very youthful appearance, a playful personality and I can act like a goof. Those qualities help me get along real well with drunks.

Not surprisingly, I discovered that I was most tempted to drink when I was losing money. I'm a conservative gambler, and I knew that drinking wouldn't help make gambling any more fun and that it wouldn't change my luck for the better. I was dying to take part in some "vice" - drinking, smoking, chewing tobacco, tax evasion, anything! I also wanted to meet some women, but I wasn't filled with "liquid courage" so I didn't introduce myself to anyone. How stupid of me was that? Here I am in Vegas and I'm not talking to women. I am in the perfect environment to tell them anything, and I have every right to do so, but I don't. The other sight that made me sad, depressed, lonely and wanting to drink was seeing all of the other couples enjoying one another. I used to be like that and I wanted that back. The most important part about my trip was that I accomplished my goals... I had fun, acted normal and stayed sober. This was a huge test for me because I experienced another part of my drunken past life as a sober person, and made it through completely unscathed.

(*February 22, 2007*) I not only suffer from the depression of losing my friend alcohol, I also suffer from the depression of losing my wife. I have read so many books by recovered addicts, alcoholics and books about coping with divorce. So many of these books talk about how the author "learned all about themselves and life is so much more rewarding now." They're blowin' smoke up your ass. Life is what it is. I will not insult you with lies or false promises of joy and happiness if you stop drinking. Life as a recovering alcoholic is a tough existence with all the temptations, self-pity, self-doubt, anger. I *feel* like my life was better when I was drinking and when I was married, or at least that's what my memory tells me. Maybe your life will take that dramatic turn for the better. Wouldn't that be wonderful?

(*March 16, 2007*) I am still so sad, depressed and lonely. I am at a loss for words in trying to explain how sad and empty I feel. I can only imagine it is like losing your spouse to death. My gregarious personality and inner strength can't pull me out of this. I wish this sensation upon no one. There is no desire to stay awake. I force myself to sit and write even this. I have felt this way for 18 months. I am so numb, so flat. I only desire sleep. I wouldn't mind getting drunk, but I fear that then death would not come soon enough. I am tired of sadness and emptiness. I guess this is the tough time? Why can't I have anger towards my ex-wife for what she did to me instead of sadness at the loss of her? I am more devastated over losing my wife than I am over quitting drinking. Going without liquor is easy. Going without my Princess is agonizing. I can't even come close to describing what I feel like. I have never *not wanted to live*, but that is how I feel now. I know that my life should be my own and I should not be defined by another person. I was so deeply in love, but I guess I fucked it all up. I know it takes two people, but I am a smart man and I should have seen the problems coming and I should have done something about it sooner. Aw fuck, who cares?

(*April 2, 2007*) I sit writing, surrounded by books, surrounded by my pets that love me. I have food, shelter, clothes, my health. My friends and my pets can make me happy for a few moments, but I continue to die inside. The wrenching of my heart is too much. I can hardly think straight. Once I do get Jessica out of my mind, she comes rushing back in. I can't sleep. I dream about her. I take sleeping pills just so that I don't dream, or at least can't remember my dreams. However once the Ambien wears off, I am tormented by the nightmares of Jessica cheating on me, being mean and heartless towards me. Then I experience guilt about my affair with Lorna am I any better than my ex-wife? I am a grown man, I am not supposed to be so emotional. I am supposed to be stoic. I have every right to be angry. By all logic I should be angry. Look at the evidence. My wife didn't want to go to counseling to salvage or work on our marriage. She didn't help me in my effort to sober up. She had an affair while we were still married and while we were supposedly "letting the dust settle." The pain and torture of living through sobriety pales in comparison to the life draining hurt I feel at the failure of my marriage. How can I allow another person's actions to affect me this adversely?

(*April, 27, 2007*) I haven't been able to determine if my luck has gotten worse since I quit drinking or if I'm just more sensitive and aware of adversity. Today just seemed like one of those days where whatever I touched I broke and nothing went right. It's days like this when I wish I had that unquestioning faith that there is a God that loves me and will help me through this. However, God is not going to fix my computer, pay my mortgage, or help me find cheap health insurance. My string of inconveniences and mishaps are purely coincidental and there is a tangible reason for every one of them. Now is when I would turn to beer or Scotch to forget my problems. These irritating inconveniences have given me a better understanding of the phrase "live in the moment."

For me to "live in the moment" I have learned that what I must do is stop my thoughts and analyze them. Are these real conditions that I am thinking about or am I watching scenes from a stage play that hasn't even been written yet? For example, I might start thinking about people that I'm mad at or thinking about drinking. These thoughts will only depress me, get me anxious, then my mind will race. I might start pacing, sweating, my heart might start beating faster, bringing on a panic situation within myself. I'll work myself into a nice panic attack, and for what? All of my anxiety and anger won't help me get my revenge on anyone. It won't change my situation, no one will suddenly come knock on my door and hand me an envelope with a coupon valid for three wishes.

My anxiety, sadness and depression is self induced. I stop and acknowledge this. I force myself to consciously control my own thoughts and activities. I cannot sit idle. My own sanity is at stake. I have no alternative other than to take control of my thoughts.

I must have faith in my decision to live sober. I truly believe that the torture I live now is far less painful than the torture I would feel if I were to start drinking again.

(*June 15, 2007*) My friendship with my dad was becoming rich and fulfilling. We really began getting to know and respect one another. Dad was living in an Assisted Living center and I would visit him a few times a week. My dad was always getting sick and being admitted to the hospital for a few days. He would have bouts with pneumonia and had some weird intestinal virus. He would always rally and get sent back to the Assisted Living center, only to get sick again a week later and be readmitted to the hospital. He was one of my best saving graces when it came to my sobriety. Whenever I felt like I couldn't make it another day or another hour sober, I would sit and talk with him. Sometimes we would say the Lord's Prayer together. That was his favorite prayer and praying with him made him feel good. He supported me and helped me feel strong and proud at what I was accomplishing. He was very hurt by Jessica. He really loved her as a daughter, but he felt that what she had done to me was unforgivable. He wanted me to stay away from her and get my life started all over again. What hurt him even more was that she lived about two blocks from him and she never went to visit him, except for the day after we divorced. He didn't speak ill of her, but he felt I wasn't being a "man" because I kept helping her out and kept seeing her.

At the end of May he was sent back to the hospital and I visited him every day. On Friday night, June 1st, I stopped by to visit. He was expecting to be released on either Saturday or Monday, depending on how his condition progressed. We had a pleasant visit, but he must have known something. He said "Jessica is not my daughter-in-law and she's not your wife any more. Stay away from her, and I don't want her at my funeral." I agreed just to humor him. In a brief moment of sincerity, I promised my dad that he could rest assured that even after he was dead, I would never drink again. We both have a sick sense of humor and I would say, "Don't go dying on me until I get back." The nurses would look at me kind'a strange, then my dad would snicker. I went home that night figuring that the next time I would be visiting him would be back at his Assisted Living home.

The next morning around 10:00a.m., my sister called me and said that I needed to get to the hospital - dad had taken a dramatic turn for the worse. She had just been called by the doctor and she wasn't sure how serious this was. She explained to me that his intestinal virus had gotten worse overnight and the doctor wanted to do surgery to remove his colon and some other parts. The doctor wasn't too confident that dad would live through the surgery but wanted us there to help decide what to do.

I drove like hell to get to the hospital. When I arrived at his room, the nurses were rolling his bed out to get him transferred to the I.C.U. Dad had insisted on having a D.N.R. bracelet (Do Not Resuscitate). From what I was told, my dad "acked out" while the doctor was discussing the procedure with him, so they put a breathing mask on his face. Boy was he pissed! Even with the oxygen mask on, my dad was gasping for air. Every breath was a struggle. He had this mask on his face and he was fighting so hard to breathe that he couldn't talk.

Once he was set up in the intensive care unit, the surgeon took us to a private room to talk. He explained that he didn't think our dad would live through the surgery. If he did survive, he would be on a ventilator tube for the rest of his life. I am appreciative at how honest, yet compassionate the surgeon was. He said that if they did nothing, he would most likely be dead by morning. He gave us some options:

#1) Have the surgery done. He may not even live long enough to prep for it and if he does have the surgery he most likely won't recover anyway.
#2) He was drowning in his own fluids and needed to be intubated to keep him breathing. They could do that and maybe keep him alive for another day.
#3) Remove the mask and let him die.

Dad told us numerous times in the past that he didn't ever want to be kept alive.

My sister and I talked to dad and told him what was going on. He could hear us but he couldn't speak. I could see terror, anger and calm in his eyes. We asked what *he* wanted. He raised his arm and pointed to the D.N.R. bracelet on his wrist. I said, "Dad, you better not be fuckin' around, this is it, there ain't no comin' back!" He kept pointing to the bracelet. Then he pointed to his other wrist. He wanted his wrist watch. I put his watch on for him. He kept checking it every few minutes.

We called for a priest. Dad received the "Last Rights". Together we held hands and said the Lord's Prayer. I held his right hand, my sister held his left hand. Foam and nasty shit was gurgling up out of his mouth. My sister would move the mask and wipe his face. The nurse came in and started a morphine line on him. They removed the mask. I said to him, "It's okay to go dad... you're working too hard... it's okay to go." I promised him for the last time that I wouldn't ever drink again. He kept checking his watch. I can only imagine that he was thinking, "Holy shit, how long does it take to die?"

It took about an hour for him to die. At 4:10p.m. June 2, 2007 my dad passed away. I was holding his hand. I got to say goodbye to him. It was not a pretty death. He did not just quietly fade away. Death is not pretty. As traumatic as it was, I will always be thankful that I got to be there when he left. I feel no guilt for the decision my sister and I made. I know it was dad's wish.

The dollar bill story: Every year at Thanksgiving I would make $1.00 bet with my dad. He bet that he would be dead before Christmas and I bet that he wouldn't. I always won, until 2007. Right before they closed his casket, I paid him. I slipped a dollar bill up inside the cuff of his shirt. He was interned with full Military honors and I was presented the flag. A few days after the funeral I took my little dogs out for a walk down a wooded and secluded road along the lake. I just wanted to take the dogs out and think about my dad. As I walked along the edge of the woods, squirrels were running around and my dogs wanted to chase them. As I walked a little further into the woods I spotted something. Sitting on top of some leaves was a single dollar bill. It was not very worn, dirty or wet, yet it had rained the night before. I took the bill home and placed it behind the death certificate, which I have framed in my office. I don't believe that the dollar bill was directly from my dad, it just seemed eerily strange in some fashion. I tell myself, "Dad was proud that I paid my bill, so he returned the favor."

Three days after dad died, I had to have my 12 year old Doberman, Eva, put to sleep. She had a similar condition. She was drowning in her own fluids. I was scheduled to take her to the vet at 5:00p.m., but she had gotten worse. Fluid was flowing from her mouth and she couldn't breathe or walk. I called the vet and brought her in at 10:00a.m. They administered the shot while I held her in my arms. If there was ever a time when someone deserves to get drunk and forget, that was it. I've held true to the promise I made to my dad. I haven't had a drink.

(*June 24, 2007*) Isn't this all fucking great? I quit drinking and I lose my wife, I lose my house, I lose my health insurance, I have no retirement, I lost all the dreams my wife and I had planned out. My career was going down the toilet, I felt weak, I was always sad, the house that I was living in was a mess, my life was a mess, my life seemed overwhelming and chaotic. In a nut-shell, my life fell apart when I quit drinking. It didn't fall apart *because* I quit

215

drinking. I think that 32 years of drinking and living the high life had finally caught up with me and it was time to pay my bill. I had to pay back 32 years of partying in a matter of a few months, so the payment of misery and agony was highly concentrated.

My situation may be very different from yours. You might be in a loving marriage with a partner that is thrilled to help you stop drinking. You may be in a volatile relationship that you can't wait to get out of. Being sober will open some new doors. All of these doors won't be pleasant.

No matter how much I whine, complain, bitch, cry and grumble, I am ultimately glad that I am sober. It is a very confusing spot to be in. I wish I could drink, I'm glad I don't. I'm sad, lonely, depressed, but I feel good that I can control my drinking. I may not always be able to control my thinking, but I can control my actions.

It doesn't matter what you have been through, what has been done to you, or what is said to you - there are NO valid reasons to start drinking again.

(*July 17, 2007*) At this writing, I have been sober for over 20 months. I have not had a single relapse. Relapses are not allowed. I have heard the stories of people who relapsed 5, 10 or 15 times before they finally quit. Relapse is NOT an option. If you're going to drink, then drink and get drunk. If you're not going to drink, then DON'T. Yup, it's that simple.

I had been thinking about trying to be a social drinker again; however I don't want to think about it too much because thinking about it is a dangerous thing for me to do. I could easily talk myself into attempting to be a social drinker. But I NEVER was a social drinker, so how could I do that now? I'm not seriously considering letting myself drink. I am doing this as a mental exercise so I solidify my decision that I can never drink again.

As I was doing my mental gymnastics, I realized that if I wanted to enjoy my drinking, I couldn't control my drinking. If I were to control my drinking, this wouldn't be fun. In fact it would be pure torture to watch as everyone else could have as much or as little as they wanted, and I couldn't. So fuck it, why drink at all and spare myself the torture. But the torment and the temptation to drink again is still so strong.

Since my divorce, I have no ambition, little to no self-confidence. I feel worthless, ugly and unlovable. I wonder what's the point of being sober? I'm not having fun, this isn't great, I am in constant emotional agony, I'm depressed, sad, lonely, I hate my job, my life, myself. So why not drink? The more I think about drinking, the more depressed I become. I know how to control this, I know what I have to do, I have the answers: stay busy, work on projects, work on stuff around the house, work on my career and my job, go out with friends, go out and meet new friends and introduce myself to women. All this sounds fun and easy. Well it's not easy and it isn't that much fun when you can't get sadness, depression, loneliness and alcohol off your mind. In fact, all this shit is downright fucking painful. Being drunk or dead seems like it would be a lot better.

(*August. 8, 2007*) Here's an interesting observation I have made. When I watch others get drunk I see how they are enslaved to their addictions. I end up feeling sad for them and I am glad that I am no longer a slave. I'm not referring to the truly casual drinker or occasional smoker. I have good friends that get drunk and say dumb things or do foolish things. Sometimes they say funny and entertaining things when they're drunk. But I truly do feel sad for them - because they don't see themselves as others see them. I watch as they go from "light and giddy" to "drunk and sloppy." It doesn't happen to every one of them, but it happens to a lot of them. I am not speaking self-righteously, I'm simply stating my observation.

With all this said, I must admit that since I quit drinking, I feel

217

like I have no drive, no passion, no reward system for myself. Sometimes I feel that if I can't drink, then all I want to do is go to sleep and not wake up. This can be a very depressing and confusing state of mind to be in. But I continue to remind myself that drinking (even socially) won't make my life better - it won't rekindle my fire for life and love - it'll just make me drunk and more depressed. Which is a greater pain to suffer? Spending the rest of my life drunk and floundering - or battling to stay sober (which ultimately gives me a chance to succeed or fail on my own merits). I truly hold hope that this is all worth it - because without hope there is no point in trying. The harsh reality for me is that I *shouldn't* and *can't* drink like everyone else.

(***December 31, 2007***) 2006 was my first full year of living sober and that sucked, but 2007 has been an even shittier year for me. I thought my life would start getting better when I sobered up. WRONG! Okay, maybe some things got better during 2007. My health improved and my thinking became even clearer, but a lot of other events happened and information surfaced that pushed me back into depression. On February 5, 2007 I found out that my wife had been having a full blown affair while we were married. Ultimately she admitted to it. She wrote me a letter telling me about it and she gave it to me on what would have been our 24th wedding anniversary. That ripped what little heart I had left into tiny shreds. And then there is the guilt of what I allowed myself to do with Lorna – like I'm any fuckin' better?

If there was ever a time I needed my wife, it was when my dad died. I was so sad and lonely. She wasn't there. My friends kept me busy and sober. A few weeks after my dad's funeral I started seeing my ex-wife again. She would invite me over for dinner or just to hang out. We even went out on a few dinner dates and had a good time together. I was still hoping for hope. I kept thinking that maybe she would ask that we try getting back together. That never materialized and it was killing me. Every time I saw my ex-wife I slipped deeper into depression and just wanted to drink myself to death. I couldn't continue doing this to myself any longer. I had to be the one to cut off all communication. I wrote a very loving note to her, explaining how sorry I was for everything bad I had ever done and how much I loved her, but that I couldn't continue seeing her if we weren't working on rekindling our relationship. I left it at her house while she was away at a horse show. She got the note when she returned. Once again I slipped back into dark depression.

Christmas this year was sad and lonely, because I missed Jessica and all the fun we would have at during the holidays. I missed my dad, missed hosting Christmas Eve at our house, spending Christmas day at Jessica's parents house. I was truly concerned that I would get so depressed that I might possibly drink. Then I thought about how lonely I was going to be, realized that I CAN'T drink and I became even more depressed. These thoughts just kept revolving through my mind and it was mental agony. Luckily I ended up getting invitations from friends to spend Christmas Eve and Christmas Day at their house. I ended up at Mike's house the afternoon of Christmas Eve. It was nice to sit and hang out with my friend again. Then I spent Christmas Eve with my sister's family at my niece's apartment. It was so wonderful to be with them. I didn't share my tale of woe. They have no idea how much they helped me stay sane and sober. Later that night I took my nephew out - of all places, to a bar - so he could have a couple of drinks.

My nephew Andy and I sat at the bar chatting. He had a couple of beers and I had a couple O'Doul's (N.A. Beer). One of the guys at the bar bought a round for everyone. I asked my nephew what he wanted and he asked for Efen Vodka. I asked for the same. Andy drank his, and then he drank mine. The reason I relay this experience is to show that you can go out to bars, even have people buy you shots and still not drink. Why should I turn down someone's gracious gift? Why try to explain to the bartender or other patrons sitting next to me that I don't drink? Why draw attention? Living a normal life, being fun to hang out with and staying sober can be done.

Now that I sit here facing New Years Eve, it's even worse. I don't feel like going out seeing all the happy couples celebrating. New Years is very depressing to me right now. Watching other people get drunk is funny sometimes. It's interesting to watch all the dynamics taking place. It makes me wonder which of those drunks I was.

(*January 3, 2008*) My friend Jhennifer came over to my house for New Years Eve, we made dinner and watched a movie. She is a wonderful friend and a wonderful woman. I wasn't alone New Years Eve, but she could tell how much I ached for Jessica. On New Year's Day I went over to another couple's house that live on the lake. I often comment to them how disgusted and repulsed I am that they are normal and happy together - they make me sick! (Naturally I am only joking - I am happy for them and envious of them.) We played darts, made dinner, joked, talked and laughed. They know my troubles and have listened to plenty of my depressing tales, but they still seem to like me anyway. Once again, good friends that have no idea how much they helped me stay sane and sober.

(*February 4, 2008*) I ended up getting divorced from the woman I loved with all my heart. We were married for 23-1/2 years. I spent more than half of my life with her, I had promised her my life. I willingly gave her my heart. She was the sweetest thing to me.

I cried for days, weeks and months on end. I cried myself to sleep for over 6 months. I would wake up crying. I had to take prescription sleeping pills so I could turn my brain off. I would go to bed every night and pray to a God I didn't believe in, that my wife would "wake up" and want me back in her life. My dearest of friends told me that I had to get over her. They told me how they could see the pain in my eyes. I was obsessed with her. Not in a weird "stalker" way, but in a way that I just couldn't get her out of my mind and let go of her. This obsession became extremely unhealthy for me. My stomach would churn, I would only think about her. I would have vivid dreams of her dating other men. It was killing me. I wasn't eating properly. I didn't care about my own health. I would get into a melancholy funk and be unemotional in my daily life. I would daydream about her while I was driving, then I would start crying and I would be a danger on the road... I wasn't paying attention to what I was supposed to be doing.

I continued to think about her and buy her things at the store. I was finally making some good money and I wanted to treat her like she claimed I never treated her. I wasn't trying to "buy her back," I just loved her and wanted to do nice things for her. I felt bad about what I supposedly had been before our divorce. I held on to a hope that we would get back together. We talked every day, 3, 4, 5 times a day, before we were divorced, even for months after we were divorced. She wasn't tormenting me on purpose - I just kept putting myself back into the torture chamber. I compare it to putting your own hand in a blender, then going back the next day and putting it back in the blender again and hoping it won't hurt this time.

I would buy things for her and then I would feel even worse because she wouldn't call to thank me. Why should she thank me? I was the one buying stuff - she wasn't asking me for it. She didn't want to live with me, she didn't want to have sex with me, she even told me that she wasn't attracted to me. She said, "I love you, I'm just not in love with you." Why in the fuck would I keep holding on when she didn't want me anymore? She was the person that had hurt me the most and I still couldn't get over her. I kept crying and asking why I couldn't get over her?

My friends urged me, advised me, virtually pleaded with me to let go of her. They told me not to take her calls, not to keep buying things for her and doing things for her. We were divorced and I would help her with repairs at the home I had signed over to her. Why was I such a gullible idiot? I am a strong man. I can quit smoking cigarettes, quit chewing tobacco, quit cocaine, quit smoking pot, and quit drinking. I can do all of these things on my own, but I can't seem to be able to let go of Jessica. I loved her so much. Why can't I just face reality? Maybe I am driven by my own guilt over what I did with Lorna? I knew what I had to do... I just didn't want to do it (sound familiar?). I'm a tough guy, but I cried, hoped, and cried some more. I would go a couple of days without crying. I tried to cry, but no tears came out. I cried so much that I ran out of tears. That hurts even more - when you want to cry but can't.

I was numb. I had to figure out why I couldn't let go. I had to talk myself into letting her go. I had to devise a plan to do this. I had to come to the harsh, ugly, painful realization that I would never have my Baby-Doll again. We were over, divorced, no longer a couple, an ex-parrot (that's a Monty Python joke). This was going to be harder to talk myself into and accept than when I realized I would never be able to drink again.

I had changed my life so drastically for the better that I kept thinking this would all be over soon and there would be a fairy-tale finish and happy ending. A happy ending my ass! That ain't how life works. Sometimes it doesn't go as planned. I had to remind myself constantly that "bad luck" and bad occurrences are nothing personal against me. God and the universe does not conspire against me to bring me bad luck. I believe that God is a little too busy to worry about making my life inconvenient, and it's grandiose, delusional thinking to imagine that the universe would go out of its way to fuck with me.

I encountered some really bad times about 2 weeks after my divorce. I had almost been sober 1 full year, another 20 days and I would make it. I kept putting myself in the torture chamber of seeing Jessica. I loved her so much and I couldn't let go.

We had made plans for her to come over to what was now "my house" after work. She came over, but she had to leave before 7:30 because she couldn't drive after 8pm because of her drunk driving ticket. I was foolishly hoping that she would just spend the night with me. I once again had all these hopes and wishes that *this* would be the time she would change her mind. I was hopeless. Anyway, she came over and we did household chores together. Silly, simple stuff like washing windows, cleaning screens on windows, etc. I kept making sexual innuendos and invitations. She was very affectionate back towards me, she even asked me to rub her back, with my hands under her sweat shirt. I kept thinking this would be the start of romance. It wasn't. After all the back rubbing just came some hugging and a kiss goodbye. As she was leaving I made a comment like, "Maybe next time you'll stay," or something like that. She just looked at me real weird. I couldn't tell what that look meant.

After she left I just sat in my recliner and stared, then I started crying, hard. My mind began to race, I couldn't figure out why I keep doing this to myself. I can't take this any longer, I want a drink! And did I ever want a drink. This was bad. I truly thought about drinking. I couldn't do this to myself. I went and laid in my bed and cried. I got up and paced around the house crying, my mind racing all the time. I couldn't think straight, I didn't know what to think, I wished that I could be asleep at that very moment. I wanted to drink so I could sleep. I laid in my bed again, I got up and paced some more, my legs were weak, I stumbled around my house, pacing, crying, I sat down on my kitchen floor in the corner of some cupboards and cried. I truly didn't want to go on any more, I didn't know what to do, I hated myself because I couldn't drink. I hated myself because I wanted to drink. I begged God again: "please God... help me." Help me what? Then I started telling myself, "never quit, never give up hope, never quit, never give up hope." I had no idea what I was hoping for or what I didn't want to quit doing.

I reminded myself of all the people that helped me to sober up and helped me get through my toughest times. I couldn't let them down; they had all spent so much of their own time and energy on me. I reminded myself of all the people that believe I'm strong. I couldn't let those people down. I wanted to drink again. All I could

223

think about was drinking or taking a sleeping pill and passing out. Suicide had crossed my mind, but I knew I wouldn't take action on it, I just wanted to escape from my own mind and my pain. I cried even more. Why do I feel like this, why must my mind hurt so much? I knew that crying wouldn't change any thing. I knew that I could cry all I wanted, but nothing would come from it. I hated everything. I was so sad. I wanted to call someone, anyone to help me through, but I had called these people enough times, I needed to *call on myself* this time. I forced myself get up and do something productive. I went to my computer and continued my writing project. I couldn't think straight at first, I just began writing - boy this sucks…

****

My journal entries end at this point because I began focusing my writing efforts on this book and material for my website. There are no dates on the short prose and essays - I have no record of when each of them was written - most were done over the first eighteen months of my sobriety. Much of what you have just read may appear confusing and contradictory to my positions on positive self-esteem. But that is an example of the confused mind during the recovery and healing process.

After four years of sobriety, I can say that I feel better, I think clearer, I do like myself and I am glad that I am sober.

My closing thoughts:

I can't stress enough, that if you think you have an alcohol or drug problem, then you probably do have a problem. Don't end up like me – don't wait until it's too late. I lost the greatest thing that ever happened to me in my life, I lost my wife. I cannot blame "the alcohol" for what happened. I made the choice to drink and to continue drinking in a Super-Human fashion. I live with that guilt every day. I am still tortured with nightmares. How could I have fucked up such a wonderful thing? I understand what I did, I accept what I did, and I can't do anything to get back what I lost. However I can have hope for a better future.

This will be the toughest choice you make in your life. It will not be easy. It can be done.

A smart person learns from their mistakes, but a smarter person learns from someone else's mistakes. Please learn from the mistakes I made as a drunk. Save your marriage, save your relationships, save your job, save your money and save your own life.

I wish you success at whatever you decide. May your life become calm, enjoyable and drama free.

Mark.

Afterword:

By - Mark A. Tuschel 2012

I would never go back and change what I have written in this book. It isn't polished, classy or very good writing for that matter – it reflects the emotions and what happens *to* and *within* the mind of a healing alcoholic. Three years have passed since the release of this book. There is so much more that I've learned in these three years and so much more that I wanted to add. Instead of rewriting the book I have put together this afterword.

Do I have any regrets for sobering up? None. Oh sure, I lament some of my decisions I've made along the way. I made plenty of mistakes and made some poor choices over the past six+ years. I am disappointed by how some things turned out, but I have no regrets.

My biggest mistakes: I spent too much time crying over my failed marriage and suffering with emotional pain – self-induced pain. I spent far too much time feeling bad about myself, feeling like I was "flawed, defective and worthless." Not that all of my past behavior can simply be forgiven and forgotten. Consequences of my past must be paid – my life is a result of what I have done.

I was also under the mistaken impression that because I *was* a drunk that I am a bad person. I am **not** a bad person and neither are you. I just drank too much. By living sober today I can be the person that I like, which helps me stay sober tomorrow.

I wish I could spare you some of the pain that you will go through. You will have to walk this path in your own shoes. We can walk it together, you can lean on me and others, but you will have to make this walk yourself.

I wish I could tell you that everything will work out fine for you. I wish I could offer you a guarantee of sober happiness. I wish I could tell you that it gets easier with time, that the temptations go away, that the struggles disappear, that all memories fade. They don't – at least not for me they haven't - but maybe this will be easier for you.

I wish a lot of things turned out different during my drinking past and over the last six years of sobriety, but they didn't, so I must plan to make things different and better in my future. I accept that all my future plans will not come together as I hope. Many things will go on and take place behind the curtain of life; I won't see them happening. I wish I could see all the good that takes place – so I could appreciate it more and thank those who directly help and support me.

While I don't have everything I want (and never will), I feel very lucky and fortunate. I will be bold and say that I have created my own good fortune and good luck because I created my own sobriety. Yes, many other people are instrumental and helpful and I am grateful to them, but only I have been the one to develop myself into the type of sober person that others want to associate with. Of course I sound arrogant. But I have gotten to be liked and respected because I treat others with respect and dignity.

As a drunk, I liked me because I didn't have to deal with me. As a sober person I must step back and ask some very serious questions about myself: "Would I want to hang out with this individual? Do I respect this person?" These two questions help me better understand why others DO or DON'T want to hang around me or respect me. If I want to be treated better by other people what do I need to change about *my own behavior*? How must I act and treat others? I don't have to be liked but I do want to be respected and I will earn your respect.

The easiest way to stay sober: Get locked up in solitary confinement or become a prisoner in your own insulated, closed off world. I feel that's what surrounding yourself with program people is like. You limit your association with the rest of the world and stay within a closed environment. All you hear is the same stuff, over and over again: "Admit that you're flawed. The steps will work if you work them. Let go and let god. You have to accept a higher power. Have I told you how weak and awful you are? etc." I never wanted that in my life and I don't want that now. I would rather deal with temptation, struggle with self-control and enjoy all that life has to offer than surround myself with what I consider a cult (well, some members are only borderline cultists).

Participating and following AA might be good for you and you might like it, but remember: **You** are still the one doing all the work. You can support the ideals, work the steps, embrace a HP, whatever, but take credit for what **you** are doing for yourself.

It's okay to be YOU. It's okay to do your own style of sober living. One size does NOT fit all. Don't be fooled into a false belief that following a certain program, religion or cult will solve all of your problems. YOU have to work on making your own life better. Living sober sucks, but I can honestly say that living life without problems, challenges and struggles would suck as well.

Without hesitation I can say that the small inconveniences of daily life are more challenging and threatening to my sobriety than the big problems. One small turd floats up in the punchbowl, then another, then another and I let that shit get to me. The small stuff fucks with my thinking more than the major problems. Those little annoyances weaken my resolve. They don't break my resolve, but I let my own thoughts exaggerate their importance. When one small thing happens it makes the next small thing seem bigger. I start thinking, "Oh this is rough. Why is ALL this shit happening to me?" That's when I question whether it's worth the effort to maintain my sobriety. I must then follow my own advice and STOP – stop my over-thinking of everything and stop my feelings of self pity. Ahhh, but then my mind fucks with me even more, "Well you stopped all your negative thinking Mark. Where did it get you? Nothing's going right anyway,,, so why not drink, what's the difference?" Ooooh you evil sneaky mind. Then, just when I think everything is going fine, somebody comes along and throws a brick through the living room window of life. That's the way it is for all of us.

On the positive side, every time I feel like I am at the end of my rope someone comes along and stretches the rope out for me. I believe that the only reason people are so willing to help me is because I am still sober. Not because I simply "don't drink," but by living sober I have become a more credible person. When I say "credible" I am not inferring that I am a warm, wonderful person to be around – fuck no. Plenty of people don't *like* me as a person but they respect and trust me as a person. They see that I am dedicated to my own sobriety and that causes them take me seriously, which in turn, causes them to want to be of help to me in my life. I'm sure it doesn't hurt that I want to be of help to other people as well. I make certain that I always give something worthwhile in return for their help. It's rarely money that I give – as crazy as this sounds – there are some things more valuable to people than money.

I have also discovered the invaluable benefits of having a goal statement. Clearly and descriptively writing out the things that you **want** and **don't want** out of sobriety will give you something to fall back on when the tough days show up.

You must stay active with your goal list; you must consistently read it and continuously update it. Goals are fluid and changing because conditions and life changes, your desires and requirements change. By writing out goals, and starting to work towards their accomplishment, I have discovered that some goals I actually didn't need or want. This has been beneficial in understanding what is truly valuable to me in life. For instance, sometimes I want something so badly that I'll forsake other goals or responsibilities, then, once the objective is reached, I find that I didn't need or want it after all. So changing goals is not a sign of weakness, changing your principles is the weakness.

A goal list, followed with an activity list, has helped me accomplish more in the six years that I've been sober than I thought I could ever possibly do. And even if I only reach half of my goals (or half of a specific goal), that's better than not reaching anything; 50% is a lot better than 0%. One goal sparks another goal and that leads to more desire, which ultimately keeps me busy and keeps my mind off of drinking. I also know that drinking again would derail all the work I've done towards attaining goals. By default, I end up becoming more skilled and gaining more knowledge as I pursue goals. So even if a goal is never reached I am always gaining something.

Things you want: As I just mentioned, having a goal list has been powerfully rewarding for me. Yes, it's tedious and mentally taxing work to layout a goal list, but the benefits make it worth the effort. Seeing progress being made towards tangible goals really helps me maintain my resolve to stay sober. It confirms my whole philosophy on creating a reward system for yourself.

Your goal list doesn't have to only comprise of financial or materialistic items. It should include: personal growth, better relationships, expansion of knowledge and skills, a desire to further your education, to be involved in some meaningful activity, a hobby or sport. Write out your goals, then write out what activities you must do to reach those goals and determine a desired completion date for each goal. Without a completion date a goal is just a fanciful wish that will most likely never happen. If you don't reach the goal by your completion date, review what transpired, how close are you, why didn't it happen, what can make it happen sooner – then establish a new desired completion date. Just keep building and working towards goals.

Things you don't want: This is a tougher one to explain and to see progress being made. But knowing what you DON'T want, and not getting it, can be better than knowing and getting what you DO want. When your goals are: I don't want debt, I don't want useless arguments, I don't want to let people down, I don't want to be drawn into others' drama, I don't want bullshit in my life, etc., these goals become invisible – it's hard to see the results. When the drama, debts and arguments disappear, (and they will disappear) you tend to forget that you've accomplished the goal.. Not having to deal with your own guilt, embarrassments and always apologizing is a nice feeling, but it isn't as concrete as when you gain something. When stupid bullshit isn't always happening to you, you tend to forget that stupid bullshit used to always happen to you. And even if you can reflect on it and feel good about it, it doesn't seem the same as when you attain a tangible goal. For me, not having stupid bullshit happen in my life is a greater goal (and reward) than gaining anything materialistic. The absence of drama makes sobriety worth it, but it's so difficult to see the value of this absence.

This strategy is detailed out with worksheets in my other book: *Okay, I quit. Now what?*

A few other things I have learned along the way:

- Others can say and do things that hurt me, but only I can harm myself.

- You have to find your own damn keys.

- Dirty little secrets don't stay that way for very long.

- The choice IS yours.

- There is no easy way out of this.

Practice: Over the past few years I've been hanging out with a lot of professional musicians – sober musicians by the way. I'm so impressed at how much these guys (and girls) practice. They practice every day, all the time. They try new methods and try new or different instruments. But they are always practicing. That's how they get to be professionals. They don't just "start" playing one day and then become accomplished musicians in 30 days, celebrate their 30 day anniversary and never practice again. No, they work on getting better all the time.

It's commonly accepted that you become more proficient at things through practice. You **are** and you **become** what you practice or participate in daily. That's why I'm using the example of a professional musician. These people practice and work on their craft every day until it becomes natural for them.

If you daily practice being angry, bitter, nervous, frustrated, filled with sober self-pity, or **drunk** – you WILL become better at it. And when I say you'll become better at it, I don't mean that you'll get it under control – NO – you will bring MORE of these things into your life. You'll get yourself to a point where you expect these conditions to exist and they'll come naturally to you. And when they don't, you create situations or conditions for them to exist.

So here's how this relates. I believe that it's important for you to practice living your life as a sober person every day. **You need to practice enjoying sobriety.** You need to practice tolerance that others can and will drink and not feel self-pity because you don't drink. You need to practice stashing away and saving your booze money, you need to practice rewarding yourself and others and you need to practice feeling proud of what you have done for yourself by sobering up. You are solely responsible for turning yourself into a drunken mess and you are the only person who can live your own sober life. You should celebrate and make a big deal out of your sobriety – be proud. But only through practice will you be in a position to truly celebrate your life as a professional sober person.

How long do you have to berate yourself for your past? Be proud of what you are doing with your life now.

For me, staying sober is a very selfish undertaking. It **is not** all about correcting my flaws and working steps. I don't want to spend the rest of my life in meetings, working steps, etc. Instead of going to meetings and publicly pronouncing that I am "weak and flawed" I have been learning how to enjoy life as a re-invented person. I want to enjoy my own life and I want other people to enjoy me as part of their life. This isn't a wild dream or unachievable goal. People who don't drink or never had a drinking problem do it all the time. Those same people (non-drinkers) also have difficult lives. Some of those people who have never had a drink in their life can be just as "flawed and filled with defects" as we drunks.

Random musings:

1 - Gonna start living sober? Don't expect ANYTHING out of sobriety – expect EVERYTHING from yourself.

2 - People ask me for advice on how to quit drinking. There truly is only ONE simple answer – **don't drink**. However, there are numerous causes and reasons for drinking, which can be a complicated mess. I believe that there are (4) categories or "causes" for being a drunk, these are: Biological, Psychological, Geographical, Social. To win at sobriety each of these causes must be looked at and worked on. Further, each cause has a different level of influence on each individual.

Biological: This is the physical capacity for the pleasure center (frontal cortex) to enjoy and be rewarded by the chemical of alcohol. Some of us get an intense rush out of drinking; it actually makes our body feel "normal." This biological condition would be considered the disease part of alcoholism.

Psychological: The personal desire to catch a buzz. The desire to use alcohol as a way to hide from or forget about something that is or has happened. The desire to use alcohol as way to become something or someone that we are not or that we are unable to be when we are feeling inhibited (sober).

Geographical: If we live in a geographical area where excessive drinking is accepted as the norm. Some Midwestern and Eastern cities have higher populations of drinkers. Cold climates promote "huddling" and people tend to drink to give them something to do. Warmer climates and tourist areas promote the party atmosphere.

Social: Family drinking habits and the drinking habits of the people we hang out with. Educational and economic status play a role in what we drink and how much of it we drink. Our desire to fit in with our peer group. Our peers influence us more than we may care to admit.

Each of the causes that I'm writing about has its own level of intensity and influence to varying degrees with each individual. Some of us don't have the biological cravings; some don't come from a family of alcoholics. When you get an understanding of which area is the strongest cause, this will help you know where to focus your work, and therefore what you need to avoid for maintaining sobriety and beating relapse.

I talk about the various causes/reasons for alcohol misuse, but I firmly believe that the greatest influence on why we drink is due to the people we hang out with and whom WE ACCEPT as friends in our life. If I surround myself with drunks, drug addicts and boozers, what else can I expect my life to be?

3 - I privately laugh when people say, "By the grace of god I'm sober." Why aren't they willing to take credit for what they have done for themselves? What grandiose thinking makes them believe that god would show favoritism to them over me or you? Another statement that makes me cringe is, "I want to follow what Jesus

235

has planned for me." What about **your** plans or what **you** want for your life? I can understand this line of thinking; some people aren't very good at running their own lives. As I have mentioned numerous times, I would never want to dissuade someone from following their religious beliefs. But I caution the newly sober from expecting that religion will cure all of your ills and free your life of problems.

Here's a crazy thought: Why not live sober FOR the grace of your god? Why not live civil and sober out of respect and reverence for your god? Just something to consider. And just because I don't believe in a religious god doesn't mean that I live amorally or support anarchy. Plenty of people who don't believe in a deity live ethical, civil lives.

4 - A very wise-guy once told me; "Mark, nature takes care of its own shit, and pieces of shit like that will be taken care of." I know what he meant. When I surrounded myself with shit (i.e. drunks, losers, deadbeats, etc.) that's what I attracted and that's what I got more of. When I surround myself with quality people it gives me something to aspire to. I've been meeting a lot more quality people now that I'm sober.

5 - Willpower must take place BEFORE I have a drink. For people like me, willpower doesn't work after booze is in my system. That would be like me ingesting a bottle of Laxatives and trying to use my willpower to not spend hours on the crapper. Willpower cannot change or stop the biochemical effects of a substance in my system. That's why I don't ingest entire bottles of Laxatives (I don't like having a case of the Green Monkey Two-step).

6 - I've met a lot of powerful people in my life. Here's what I've observed: The most powerful, influential people - COMMAND power through respect – they don't demand power. They are strong, productive, ethical, influential and ultimately POWERFUL. The rest are a bunch of blowhard fuck-holes that push their shit down everyone's throat. They may be feared but they are not powerful.

7 - Out of all the states I've been through, Texas has the most dead shit lying in the road. I should stop and grab some of these fine pelts. I could decorate my RV in a wild Hunter/Safari motif.

8 - Somebody told me that I seem angry and that I need to relax. What? "I give up alcohol and now you want me to give up anger, bitterness and frustration too? Fuck no! Now I can fully enjoy those emotions. "

9 - Another interesting weekend of "drunk watching." Good reminders for why I'm glad I don't drink any longer. Saturday: Watched the drunken dramas & arguments unfold. Highly inappropriate flirting and cavorting of women when their husband/boyfriend isn't with them. I'm certainly not a puritan – believe me, I like a dirty girl – but this shit was wrong! Funny to watch what people turn into after a few drinks.

Sunday: Watched Packers/Bears game at a sports bar in Phoenix. Bar tab arrives after the game.
Mine = $3 + tip
Theirs = $196 + tip

10 - What you DON'T imagine about your future can be more harmful than what you DO imagine. We typically only imagine the outcome or the "end result" and neglect to consider what happens AFTER the end result. What happens along the journey & what other consequences (good & bad) might occur. For instance, I can imagine that if I was: married, divorced, rich, the kids were grown up, 10 pounds lighter,,, I'd be happy. Really??? What happens along the way? What happens **after** I get married, divorced, kids move out, make more money, lose that last 10 pounds? Will I suddenly become happy and everything will be perfect from that point on? The things that happen **during** and **after** are more important. Unless you die – life continues after a goal has been

237

reached. We (me as well) forget to imagine the details. Imagining only the "outcome" is wishful thinking. Imagining the DETAILS is planning for success and preparing for inevitable obstacles.

11 - Too many talented people have died attempting to find their creative plane. "Junk" works as a crutch to think obscure things, but it's mostly bizarre shit, then you lose your edge. The pain AFTER cleaning up is a story more people can relate to. Kind'a hard to tell me your story when you're dead.

12 - Creativity isn't limited to art, music or writing. Creativity is how you live your life, interact with people, care for your kids, treat your partner, arrange your furniture, style your hair or how you look w/out hair. Creativity is who you are and how you act sober. Show people how creative you ARE.

13 - It sucks when,,, I get so distracted by my own brain that I forget to watch (and enjoy) the movie of "Life" playing right in front of me - complete with surround-sound, big screen and in 3-D. So I must not only experience but be aware and engaged in the experience of this movie.

14 - When I wake up, I have to go to my job and my job is to live as a sober person. The more I work at my job, the better I get at it. But like any job, sometimes I'd rather be doing something else. Some days my job sucks. So? And just like having a job, sobriety is my own personal responsibility – to show up on time, get better at what I do, further my education about my job and to do good work. I choose what job I apply for; therefore I also choose my sobriety. Nobody forces me to work, to drink or to live sober.

15 - I allowed alcohol to run my life. Being drunk on a daily basis got in the way of me performing up to the level that I know I am capable of. I felt as if I was being robbed by "bad luck." I was only robbing myself of success. Alcohol didn't do it – I did it. I had fucked myself out of too many productive years and opportunities. It came time for me to un-fuck myself.

In Summary:

Here I am, 6-1/2 years later and still sober. I am happier, wiser, more realistic and comfortable with myself. I don't expend all of my effort trying to impress or please people; attempting to be accepted and liked by other drunks, losers and deadbeats. I have a clearer head about me; I want things in life and the only way I will get them is by laying out goals, doing activities to reach those goals and continuing to live a sober life. There are still things missing in my life, but I must keep digging and looking for them. As a realist I accept harsh truths; I accept that failures and disappointments will always be a part of my life. I realize that I won't always (if ever) get exactly what I want but I am also a dreamer. Without my dreams and hopes for finding love, happiness and a rewarding existence, there would be no reason to go on. Sobriety may suck, but my chances of finding love, happiness and a rewarding existence are far better sober than drunk. So I'll keep trying and keep dreaming.

Does living sober still suck? Yes, some parts of it. Knowing that I'll never cop a buzz again sucks. Seeing in advance what situations might not be good for me and struggling to stay away from those tempting situations can be tough. Many of the drastic changes I have undertaken in my lifestyle do suck. **But my life doesn't suck.** I'm still glad I did what I did.

It is so gratifying to hear from others who have personal pride in their re-invention. I am so happy to hear someone say, "I feel good about myself and my thinking. I am happy that I am able to stay sober on my own, without giving my power over to some invisible being or some group. I have a savings account and I never had money before. I am accomplishing things in my life that I want to. Thank you for telling your story and helping me discover that it's okay to be proud of myself."

If there is anything you gain by reading this book, I hope it is the understanding that sobriety doesn't guarantee anything. But that doesn't mean it isn't worth the effort. Drunkenness on the other hand guarantees a lot of things: PROBLEMS. I could list all the probable shit that will befall you, but why? You already know.

Whether you hate me or love me, I hope that I stirred some emotions within you and have caused you to think. I sincerely hope that your sober life turns out better than you ever imagined and better than mine ever will.

Thank you for reading this book.

Mark Tuschel

Other books by Mark Tuschel:

Okay, I quit. Now what? / Becoming a Re-Invented Alcoholic

The Malingerer's Handbook - Living off the fruits of someone else's labor

Alcoholism and its treatment is a very personal and sensitive issue. I'm sorry if I pissed anybody off or ruffled some feathers.

You may contact me through my website:

www.LivingSoberSucks.com